Connecticut River Review

Connecticut River Review
2019

Connecticut River Review is a national poetry journal sponsored by the Connecticut Poetry Society. All rights revert to authors on publication.

Editor: Ginny Lowe Connors
Design: Cindy Stewart
Cover Photo: John O'Boyle

ISBN: 978-1-7335567-2-9

Contents

POEMS

PRIZE WINNERS

Connecticut Poetry Award 2018 (judged by Daniel Donaghy)

Connecticut River Review 2018 (judged by Daniel Donaghy)

Chris Abbate

Skeleton Key

Breakfast at an inn this summer—
four couples perfectly paired
around the orange tongues
of candles, the crystal fingers of
knife-rests on a white tablecloth.
They talk of the ambitions
of their grown children.
We reply *No* when they ask
if we have any;
as if we had sidestepped
this phase of adulthood,
suppressed an urge
they had solved years before.

On the porch that night,
a couple tells of the recent passing
of their son;
a disease that paid no mind
to his young family and promising career.
It seems their grief is lost
somewhere between them
and they have been trying
to find their separate ways to it.

Upstairs, each guest room
has its own name and décor;
even the floor boards emit
distinct groans under our shoes.
But I imagine the skeleton keys
for the others' door handles
are just as stubborn as ours,
until finally, I feel it catch,
and the latch gives way;
this wrought instrument of mystery
and the quiet dwellings
of our solace and sorrow.

Laura Altshul

Distance

Not far the trail to the hill
she can see from her window,
not far. They often hiked
to the top together.
Breezy up there, view
to their house below
through treetops.
Not far.

Not close either, not close
at all. Now she's confined
to the chair on wheels
by the window, confined
to the care of a nurse
and a feeding tube
and a machine she blinks
at to talk for her, each stare
a letter on the screen to spell
the word, create the sentence.
Her once busy hands stilled,
her body immobile.

He hovers nearby, unwilling
to leave. She wants him near,
wants him close but knows
he needs to go. Go, she blinks,
hike the trail for me;
get to the top and wave.

He turns on his phone and hers,
cradles hers onto her lap, dials
then answers his own call for her.
Keep the line open, and I'll keep
mine open too and you'll
be with me as I walk.

Her eyes are tired.
He fetches binoculars,
alerts the nurse.
I'm off, he says.
She hears the closing
door, his footsteps,
his breath into the phone
in his flannel breast pocket
as he strides away.
He hums as he walks,
and talks into the phone,
tells her of the stream
he's crossing, the rock
where once they'd paused,
and the fallen tree,
then silence, just breath
and he's gone.

Here I am!
The nurse sets the binoculars
against her startled eyes
and there he is, waving
to her and she sees him
but knows he cannot see
her.
Too far.

Carol A. Amato

Escape

Fence-sitting we wait,
trespassing in McGaffery's field.
Distant rumbling like an impending storm
the thundering gets closer
silencing the raucous crows.
Eyes to the right we jump down
and begin jogging, slowly at first
pacing ourselves then pick up speed
as it approaches: the 5:15 out of New Haven.

Trampling the leggy wheat behind us we whoop
in unison drowned out by the Lionel roar.
The engine passes and the conductor waves
in wide semicircles and we wave, too.
He sounds the usual three short blasts and passes:
box car, coal car, sometimes passengers across
intimate tables.

Breathless,
the stitches in our sides
are knitting needles threatening
to pierce our lungs with every gasp for air.
When we reach the top of Copp's Hill,
the train is already distant, a puff of
gun-metal smoke fading into the milky blue.
We throw ourselves onto the grass
and roll ignoring the rocks that will
later leave beet-red bruises
for us to admire and compare.

Still breathless
we take in the sweet-apple air
when we stop in the orchard.
We laugh and laugh and lie on our backs
pointing to quixotic cloud creatures,
telling tall tales of pirates who plunder flying
ships and conquer the treacherous shoals of sky.

We wait,
until the sun dips golden behind the hill
delaying the inevitable return to the dark
house with its stony stifled laughter
charged air
and curtained light.

Sherri Bedingfield

I Dream My Husband Returns

Hearing a whip-poor-will, I thought
of dreaming and closed my eyes.
I dreamed I was awake

but knew I was sleeping. My eyes
were open in the dream. In the dream
I was resting

on my bed in the dark dark.
No shaft of light let me see him,
but he had come

and I did see him. Had I conjured
him present in my dream? I asked
myself that while sleeping.

The air that was him became dense,
thickened around me. My husband
gathered like a fog

collected over me, in front of me.
He was the air, I could breathe him in.
My dead husband had become

a mist over my bed, a guest
at our breakfast table. He didn't speak.
I thought he would,

it could have been yesterday. In an
instant his airy weight slipped away
to hover at the doorway

then venture outside. The moon must
have pulled him. The dream faded
him thin.

Ace Boggess

Ten Years Ago

I stood mute before the judge—
head bowed as if in prayer, as if penitent—&
listened to him bellow, "Twenty-five,"
quarter century, more than a generation. Twenty-
five! I knew that number would be halved by good time,
again for possible parole. Knowledge
didn't erase the sound of it like hellfire promises

from the ugly clergy. I'd been damned, condemned,
cast off like a sock with holes.
I entered the courtroom in suit & tie,
left in shackles like Jean Valjean before his last escape.

I acted much less literary, bought my ticket to grief
with blood. I lifted knives. I spoke the threat,
though muffled in my private language of fear &
desperation, an argot in which the word for sorrow
is silent, word for regret more a sigh
or noisy scratching from another room.

Daniel Bourne

Autobiography with Line Breaks

I

I press this paper down
Imagining my father scribbling
With his finger on his knee
Counting acreage and drought,
The math that could not feed us
On that farm he had to sell.

Carter Bourne wrote with his left hand.
He stuttered, words beating like the wings
Of a captured sparrow.
The runt of his litter,

He was not just the youngest son.
He could not hold the twisting horns of his farm.
He could not wrestle the growing weeds of cancer.

II

Youngest son of a youngest son,
No wonder I tried to be a poet,
Another awkward farmer.
There is pigweed and mares-tail everywhere

But I won't sell my land just yet.

This is why I still open my mouth.
On the page, there is no stutter.
On the page, the farm can flourish.
On the page, my dad still lives.

On the page I plant things.
Straight rows I hope
Will intersect with distance.

Roxana Cazan

Your Name Is Cornelia or Half-Elegy for Illness

Having fallen so hard, three quarters of the way,
having lost your balance right at the very

end of the soar across the threshold,
having felt so terrible and undeserving,

like everything was so unfair—a steal of gifts,
a wilted soar across the threshold—

and all these faces floating above your bed
like they were there to stay,

having peaked over the brink of night
and felt this falling from up above,

this unraveling from the high history
of your regal name, you stumbled into this stiff

stage of life like a debutante in dementia,
you traded your excellent pedigree for some feathers

in your hair, but not like Vermeer had intended,
no breasts lolling, fusing desire with men's lust

in an ideal 17th century, for example,
but old and frizzled by all the happening & all the hurt.

And despite your name, there's nothing noble about it,
not right now, in this rented bed,

in this new room
that looks to you more like a shed

built poorly along the banks of a river,
this cruel severance as if a heavenly remote

control muted you, trashed your legacy,
thinned your Roman blood, and splayed you

across this bed like a paralyzed Christ,
like the hollow half of a walnut,

you're ticking towards the unusual
having looked away from the light,

but your bones and teeth are still churning DNA,
and the heart inside the church of your chest

is still taking to water.

Lauren Coggins

By the Fistful

When I see the currency
of spring blowing—

those cherry blossoms aloft
like so many dollar bills

in a game show booth—
they remind me of you.

Of how I want to be
that contestant, given a minute

to grab for all I'm worth,
and win by the fistful.

To stuff my pockets, my socks,
my shirt, to feel against my chest

something drawn, impossibly,
from the air.

Lauren Coggins

Fourth of July

The call and response
of the neighbors' fireworks is jazz
percussion, staccato notes

like soloists—erratic, bursting
in the cloudy sky. I never cared
for jazz. Those odd breaks

and hanging phrases
like conversations with my father,
when neither of us knew

what to make of my growing up.
Like a storm on the Fourth of July,
when the menace of a heavy horizon

hurries revelers inside,
carrying plates of interrupted dinner
and forgetting what it was

they might have said,
their words running too
in the fluent rain.

Ken Craft

Mystery

When I was a boy, they were simply sounds of summer:
the faraway buzz of a chainsaw,

the drawn-out drone of an airplane,
the stridulation of cricket wings in fields of wildflowers.

Somewhere, a block or more away, the bark of eternal dog.
And the fading wheels of trucks, rubber

memorizing interstate from New England to Florida.
Voices close enough to hear, far enough to wonder about.

High winds swaying white pines, maples, oaks,
how it sounded like surf looking for its ocean.

Someone's lawnmower. A woodpecker rapping dead wood.
And when it came, rain on macadam, a metal roof,

downspouts and bluestones at their base. The mystery?
When summer sounds became lonely ones.

Barbara Crooker

Equinox

And another year goes up in smoke:
crab apples, horse chestnuts, russet
pears. Shadows lengthen when
the sun goes down, a couple of notches
earlier each night. Colors shift, become
ample, supple. Summer has rowed
away from the shore. Husks, rusks,
seed pods, casings. We want to beg
the sun to stay, tug on it with a golden
rope in both of our hands. We want to delay
the bleak inevitable, want to linger in
the bright garden even as the frivolous
petals start to let go.

Kika Dorsey

Tiffany, the Sirens

Your home in LA is ocean, sand, and sun
and you gave birth to four children
with your womb of eternal summer.
Your children surf when the tide
is gentle enough to carry them,
tumultuous enough to move them,
while my children climb rocks
and collect coats for winter's white cold.
When I visit you, the beaches stretch
like our memories of Lamaze class,
where we counted our breaths and pushed.
We are still pushing.
But Tiffany, you do it with more grace.
If I had four children
I would not be able to catch them if they fell.

Once I smoked Thai Stick in high school
during lunch break, then went to P.E.
We were dancing and stretching legs
and there was a disabled girl with crippled legs
struggling with the moves, and I saw
the black plane we were balancing on,
and she was slipping beneath it.
I wanted to hold her up, but I was high,
and I was playing the game as best I could,
and I stretched my arms and moved my legs
on that black plane, and I thought of leaving
the school with its chalk, lockers,
with its bored teachers and fist fights at lunch.

Now we have teenagers with perfect legs
and minds as sharp as the LA sun.
They plunge into the Pacific
while we visit the Getty Villa.
I linger at the statue of Orpheus
and the two sirens.

Their mouths are shut because his song was enough,
and their bird legs are as thin as my hope
to save this planet.

Tiffany, I never feel that my song is enough.

The vines and berries on Dionysius' head
crown the summer sky, and though he is my god,
I worry I love wine too much.
I like it red like blood.
When I bleed, I think of our wombs,
how we can pocket the future
and branch across this thin plane,
waving like the sea.

You balance on rise and breach.
I tread water and dive under waves
when they get too big.
Sometimes the dolphins dance near us,
arched like the diving back of God.
Our children never asked us how to swim,
but we taught them anyway.
Now they cool themselves in the ocean
from this hot, smoggy world.
From a distance it looks like a flat plane,
but when the body enters water,
every tug and push and ripple labors
to bring us to shore,
even when the sirens sing.

Anna Elkins

The Poet Enters the Nun's Castle

I.
The plums ripened *while I was beseeching the Beloved.*

II.
I pulled them from the tree, asking it to *give us understanding of the magnitude.*

III.
The tree answered when I bit into its stone fruit: *we are already blessed.*

IV.
Gathering. Pitting. Cutting. Baking into cobblers for friends.
Remember: *the important thing is not to think much but to love much.*

V.
What is the hope of every plum & person? *Perfect union.*

VI.
When I was six, I tried to dye the green plums purple. *I wish I could say more about this, but it is ineffable.*

VII.
After the ripening, the first frost. After the frost, the freezer full of plums. *I confess that I am deeply confused.*

Italicized text from *The Interior Castle*, St. Teresa of Ávila, Translation by Mirabai Starr. Riverhead Books. 2003.

Anna Elkins

The Poet Bakes the Nun a Plum *Galette*

These are the facts of the imagination, the very positive facts of the imaginary world. —Gaston Bachelard, *The Poetics of Space*

Dear nun who loved cooking & eating & believed God also lives among the pots & pans: I cordially invite you to tea. Can you accept? My doubt's not for how far the travel—oceans & centuries are relative—but more for your cloistered life. Still, you're fully spirit now, so maybe you can come. I'm making something lovely with plums. I keep my freezer full of them—pitted, halved, ready. O the way crust meets fleshy body of baked fruit. The magic of it: This is the only plum *galette* that will ever be made with these plums on this day by these hands lifting in pastry-dusted praise. & I'd guess this to be the only plum *galette* ever offered to you from the close & distant future.

Chris Espenshade

Driving East Out of Corning

Chemung and Susquehanna, rivers
Tioga, Chenango, Otsego, and Chemung, counties
Catatonk, Owego, Unadilla, Otego,
Oneonta, Apalachin, and Schenectady, towns
Seneca and Cayuga, lakes
Place names label stolen lands,
histories no longer taught.

O.A. Fraser

Because I Knew Donnie

Because I knew Donnie,
willowy, tall, thin,
mock angry face,
playful, pouting grin
I know sadness.
I know emptiness within.

Because I knew Donnie,
red late afternoon eyes,
full black cherry lips
and chest-heaving sighs,
I know hurt.
I know the darkened skies.

March, bury with your new snow
tulips that may never grow;
Black boys bracing your last frost,
shuffling night sidewalks
never coming home, lost.

Here a backslider, chugging gin
sucking tart slices of lime.
Drunk with desire, loving sin
dying before his time.

Again the boys before the men,
the saplings before the trees.
Is this extinction? Is this the end?
And who, who shall replenish these?

Because I knew Donnie,
long wild rope curls,
too, too baggy pants
talking trash to thick girls,
scheming for his chance,
how shall I ever talk about

the fruits of justice,
and the fairness that you tout?

I knew Donnie.
Barely a moustache on his lip
sweating over pizzas
looking for a tip,
looking for love
looking for trouble,
looking for daddy, Daddy.

The last snow
always takes young lives.
It's a bitter apple
that a cold spring survives.

Because I knew Donnie
of the dimpled chin,
you understand now
the shape I'm in.

Jennifer L. Freed

How to Hide Your Heart

In Freshman Honors English, the teacher
suggests essay topics: How to pick the perfect
outfit. Why you love
your dog.
The boy beside my daughter draws penises on his desk.
The teacher says, Be honest. Use real details
from your lives.

In World History, the class returns to the rape of Nanking.
My daughter's friend was raped
when she was ten.
This year she's been slipping, her inner balance
shifting.
Last week her mother hoped
she might be stable soon.
Last night she swallowed a pencil.

Today, a kid named Luke asked why they had to watch
the documentary about Nanking.
Why not something less unpleasant?
For a heartbeat, the history teacher held
his gaze, then said, Because
it happened.

Now, at the kitchen table, my daughter
starts an honest essay
about what happens
when she tries to sleep,

but she has no pencil sharp enough
to write what's wrong,
and she cannot shape her heart
into proper essay form.
She doesn't trust her instincts
anymore.
She doesn't trust her English teacher's eyes.
She doesn't trust the world
that will not, for all the girls in China, save her
friend from its ravages.

She is tired.

She says, Never mind.
I'll write what the teacher wants to see.

Margaret Gibson

Elegy, Immature Form

Driving the two-lane southeastern artery, early afternoon
and thwunk! what in the...a bird tumbling through
the open passenger window, mid-flight, a bird interrupted
by its impact with the edge of the car roof, interrupted
and falling into the aisle of air between car seat and door
where I can't see it—and I've seen this accident of air
and illusion before, mind-sloggering the impact on closed
window glass, a token bit of feather, a smudge, the bird
bounced onto the grass: dead on impact or if stunned
and given time, it stutters off; if lucky, it lives—so that
I'm pulling over now where asphalt meets a flush of burdock
and such—opening the car door to find the bird (smallish
blue/gray crested) enough life left in it that the claw-like feet
try to hold on to the car rug, I have it now, gentle, be
gentle, I have it in my hands, it's panting, it's in shock,
no struggle now, still breathing as I grab a folded bit of
morning newspaper and look about, leaving the weathered
tarmac, a parking area of sorts, trucks in neat rows over
there to the left—what's that smell? fetid, nose-wrinkling—
and off the man-made surfaces, onto dirt and grass, I find
in the shade of ragweed and sumac and hay stalks
a protected spot and lay the bird down—it rights itself!
it stands! so it's perhaps just stunned, but there's a rumple
at the top of one wing, a hunch that doesn't match, *water
it needs water*, so back to the car, and would you believe it
Beethoven's idling along with the motor, here's my water
bottle, no cup, no lid, no useful junk to hold the water, only
the plastic sleeve for the newspaper, perhaps it will make-do—
what is that smell rising from open tanks sunk into the ground
the lids are off—and the bird in its bower has a black round
thing in its beak, is it wounded? a gobbet of blood, or a spleen
spit up from its bird guts, looks like—well, hello—it's a berry,
pokeweed or huckleberry, and I see the bit of bright yellow
kids' rubber raincoat yellow, on the tip of the tail, diagnostic
a yellow that looks as if the tail's been dipped in paint—so,
a cedar wax-wing, but not brown, no red epaulets, it's blue-gray,

evening-shadow color, now another berry's disgorged
wax-wings eat fruit, it's a liquid the color of blueberries
made plump by heat in the pan, a summer jam blue, berries
just hot enough to pop, the liquid's that same burst of purple—
blood? or is this really fruit, I wonder, as I drop a bit of water
into its open beak, using my fingertip, another drop, and the
bird looks interested, not grateful, just a dip of the head as I
fashion the plastic into a nest shape, a basin, and pour water in—
what more can I do? there must be more, the bird will either
die from the impact or live to fly off, or a random fox will…
I pour water and turn away. Don't think about it.
On the way back to the car, finally I notice, off to the side
of the trucks, rows of portable-potties, and the odor, unmistakable,
holy shit! cisterns full of it, each with a long-handled spade
to swirl the haul of human excrement—and now I wake up
to the truth: this is no elegy, I'll never get used to it, there's no
affirmation, just berry blood and shit, and I might have done
more, what am I thinking, pulling back into traffic, leaving the scene
there's a Nature Center near, there's a vet down Shewville
on the way to Mystic—but I'm stuck in a traffic jam, turns out
yes, there's an accident, and dear reader, if you think, given
the asphalt, the trucks, the cisterns of waste, and the traffic
we're in an urban landscape with weeds thrown in, you're
wrong—it's a side-business, this shit; these are fields
fallen into disuse, old farm fields, and it all fits, doesn't it?
Cedar waxwings love berries and brush and open fields with
          thickets—
it's a gorgeously turned-out waxwing, a juvenile, what the books call
immature form, stuffing itself on berries, readying for the long and
treacherous fall migration along a diminishing trail of berries
it's the long passage home, it's the long passage home cut short…

Margaret Gibson

Reflection, Looking Straight Ahead

...meanwhile, I have to confess, mirrors
confuse me

especially the small one over the dresser
that faces
           the open bedroom door

so that, all this while, years really
brushing my hair
           choosing an earring

looking straight ahead

I haven't noticed that at least half
of the painting

over the sofa in the next room
floats
        in the mirror

a field and sky at sundown
right there

next to my face

I know that to *look* is one thing
to see, another

that it's more than a matter of angle
focus, stance—

but to think that all the while
I've been leaning in close

the painting has been there
field and sky

and noticing them now, finally
I'm drawn to consider

what else daily I live with
and don't notice

afraid to, perhaps…

As a child I'd drift into wondering
what if
                after the final

conflagration, erasure, rapture
or roiling upheaval

what if only I survive

how then would I find food, or grow it
make a brick

understand gravity, list
the elements

solve an equation, sketch an atom
hum the whole of

Beethoven's Ninth
recall a wren—

so tell me now, before it's too late

why must I pare myself down
to the last-one-left

before I admit the fields and the woods
already are silent
                as nearly

silent as they are in the painting
only partially

reflected in the mirror, where
next to my face

summer field and horizon
lie close

so close we share the same skin
the same

sun already gone down gold
behind dark cedars

leaving the sky
lit

the immense painted sky
drizzled
            with delicate

black smatter, with tiny motes
that fall on everything

equally, and I didn't notice them
before
            I didn't see them

until now here they are, falling
into a mirror
            in which

simply to see myself there
is to ask

            what to do, how to live

why must I die?

Gary Glauber

Celeste

On the rush hour 6 train
      I play a game of trying
to find whatever is blue:
clothing, eyes, advertisements,
      because life is like that.

On the platform, I see a woman
whose expression conveys
how the world will end.
But no one here has time for despair.
Here in the tunnels lacking sky
we share mass vibrations
and find ways to soothe our savagery.

      For me, it's the blue of that gentleman's shirt,
the encroaching navy of a Magritte print in that *New Yorker*,
the cerulean mystery of the jazz riff from the distant buskers,
      the turquoise teardrops of a stranger's earrings,
the color of our last salvation.

Carol Grametbauer

Still Life at Dawn

In the grass next to the playground,
a pair of black, rubber-soled
Mary Janes lie at right angles
to each other, one on its side,

one upright. Nearby, on the bank
along the creek, a blue-winged teal,
as motionless as if carved from wood.
Questions lift into the morning sky

like dew-spangled moths:
the child, her circumstances,
how the shoes were left behind;
and the duck, its loneness, its singular calm.

Gladness glows warm in late afternoon
and fades with the evening light;
by daybreak only dream-embers remain,
and a feathered sentinel standing watch.

As I pass on the path, I glance back
for one more look, the small shoes
a dark lump in white clover, the teal
at last craning its neck, gazing

into the distance, eyes fixed
on something only it can see.

Connie Jordan Green

Where I Live
after Maxine Kumin

is hardscrabble: pasture
where stones sprout each winter,
our spring harvest lines fence rows.

>I garden where clay soil's
>stubbornness is mitigated by years
>of mulch—rotted leaves, cow
>and sheep droppings, litter from
>a daughter's pen of Rhode Island reds.

I walk where generations farmed,
rose before dawn to milk and feed,
gather and groom, sweated behind mules,
beast and human equally obstinate.

>Here hawks soar, plaintive calls fill
>the June air, vultures migrate across
>October's vast blueness. Here winter
>suet feeds downy and pileated, tube feeder
>hangs with finch and titmouse.

Here the oak, and here the earth
where children smoothed roads
their toy cars traveled, where stones
lined their make-believe houses,
and minutes fled into years,
the quiet that always waited
enfolding us like a shroud.

William Greenway

The Ghost of Christmas Past

It's mostly this time of year
that I search for her
in my dreams of coming home
from college for the holidays.

Sometimes we're on our favorite backroad
in the back seat of my '53 Ford,
me doing all the work, since
I was too shy to ask.

In another dream, she was
a bank teller smiling her freckled smile
from her cage across fifty years,
as she told me she was sorry,
that my account was empty,
that I should come back another time.

Funny how long we hold on to happiness,
how long to pain.

Last night I wandered through an old folks home,
thinking I might still recognize her, though
she's an old woman by now, surely
a grandmother, if not
a great- one,
though I'm only now a father.

I've looked for her online (who
doesn't?), but I don't know how
to search for something so far gone,
though I've tried everything
I can think of about *love*:
young, first, great, only, lost.

Pat Hale

Bone and Marrow

after Standing Man with Hollow Calf, sculpture by Stephen DeStaebler

Inside the body, the bones.
Under soft flesh, mineral weight,
melding of form and function.
Hard architecture of calcium,
honeycomb of inner scaffolding,
the birthplace of blood cells.
Anatomy, science of the transparency,
spelling the grand design for us.

Given over to flame, bone and marrow
reduce to ash, coarse and rough,
riddled with remembrance:
a picnic, there, in the pine grove
by the lake. A careless cook-fire,
hot coals half-buried in the sand.

Pat Hale

To Tell One Story is to Not Tell Another

after The Birdcage, painting by Frederick Carl Frieseke

To see the blossoms pinned in a woman's hair
is to let the others bloom uncounted.
To paint parrots the green and yellow
of the flowers around them, using the same
raw swipes of paint, is to lose the birds
in a chaos of color. Only the slashes
of black tail prove the birds exist at all.
How many birds live within the cage?

To paint the woman, her exquisite spine,
is to let the parrots drift out of true.
The robe slipping from one naked shoulder
will keep her within the shelter of garden.
No passageway through the wall of flowers;
there is no leaving the beautiful cage.

A. Hampford

Catastrophic Molt

How vocal and vulnerable they are, these penguins stained
in red krill, half-feathered and huddled on the melting

snow. They grow new plumage to survive the year. Three weeks
shore bound and awkward before returning to the sea. Thinner,

cleaner. Elegant. They ignore me hovering in the slush. Fully
clothed. Leaning into no one. Staining nothing. Beneath

the layers, my skin wrinkles, roughens. Dead cells slough
off, new cells look old. Stories preserved in scars, tags, sun

spots. I can't shed any of it. I forget I'm not young, tell myself
possibilities still exist. I learn another language. Nurse

a half-hearted longing to see more—the Aurora Borealis,
Petra, an Esmeraldas Woodstar. I make lists. How many kinds

of alone are there? I want to be on fire, wet with the gak and squawk
of intimacy. Dirty dishes, morning breath, a floor that needs

sweeping. Me, aging. Naked. Tinting something. Seen.

Note: catastrophic molt is the process by which some water birds molt all of
their feathers at one time.

Max Heinegg

Memory's Alchemy

In the 23rd hour, the cord knotted, a devil's scarf
only a knife could loosen. Her heartbeat swan-dove
the screen. You never saw, as I did what the birth class taught:
say *I love you*, then   shut   the   fuck   up!

Once we signed, determined nurses spirited you into Delivery.
I waited outside, absurd in elastic booties, & my hallway walk
became the steps one takes in dreams to a field of entire light
before a sea where two swimmers are pulled, shuddering.

Then inviolate, surgical lights revealed surgeons turned
seraphic & the bloody cloths they counted vanished,
& the simple bed became the frame where forty-two weeks
of the leaden ended. Our life rested in a nest of gold.

Jenna Heller

after the argument

I go for a long walk
in search of fresh perspective
while our fighting words clatter around
and stomp up and over formidable dunes
I race right out to the water's edge
then turn and walk a jagged line
down the whole length of the beach
the incoming tide slaps my feet
each wetting wearing me down
and the uncertain fate of us, hanging
in the late afternoon sunshine
warm like believing your hand on my back
is unwavering kindness and together
we are merely a prism
with two opinions refracting
and reflecting parallel views
like the way rainbows make sense
of the sun and rain together
creating the illusion of something
only seen through distortion
and just as rare and rewarding
as dreams of our future

Paul Hostovsky

Practice

You can't even let go
of the blue casserole dish—
how in the world
are you going to let go
of the world? I ask myself,
standing in my kitchen
in the late afternoon sunlight
which is turning everything to gold.
Everything, that is, except the blue
casserole dish, which isn't here
because my stepdaughter borrowed it
without asking me.
And it pisses me off because
I love that casserole dish.
Because it belonged to my mother.
Let it go, I tell myself, or maybe
that's my mother telling me,
because she had so little time herself
to practice letting go, suddenly
finding herself on the gurney
in Emergency, apologizing
to all the nurses: "I'm sorry.
I'm not very good at this." As if
"this" were something one could
get good at, if one practiced
letting go a little at a time,
practiced dying a little at a time,
practiced turning to gold a little at a time.

Tony Howarth

Old Man Flopped on a Chair

I think I'm done with apple-picking now,
believe I'll never find the energy
to do it next year once again.
The weeks of preparation,
wheeling equipment into place.
My drooping body.
A rising chorus urges me to consider
assisted living, a way to escape the anxiety
of looking after house and garden.
But who am I if I have to walk away
from all my books, from my naps
stretched out in front of the fire,
from stepping outside at my leisure
to wander through the orchard,
greeting every tree with a finger touch,
from who I once was—a kid
sent to the police station for scrumping
in Colonel Sinnot's orchard.
I wasn't stealing, I was running free,
swept up by all his trees
and what they give us.
Years later with the help of our son
and his school mates, we cleared
the hillside and planted twenty trees.
Since then, every year, cutting the hay-high grass,
cleaning up after storms and bears,
heaving bushel baskets full of windfalls.
And next September—the joy of physical labor,
friends and family gathered for bread and soup,
apples picked and crunched into cider.

Jenevieve Carlyn Hughes

Blessed Are We

What is the world?

Child, the world is an oyster,
And you are its pearl.
Precious gift of the sea.

(Blessed are we).

But what is the sea?

Child, the sea is life's song,
And the tide is its rhyme.
A lullaby to you from me.

(Blessed are we).

But who might you be?

Child, I am the Moon,
The Mother-of-Pearls.
Guardian-keeper of tides.

(Blessed am I).

For the world is an oyster,
And you are a pearl.
And you and the world
are mine.

(Blessed am I).

David Hummon

Appendectomy

It's so good to get my body back,
like climbing into the old Camry, knowing I will get there and back.

Hard when it's in for repair. They don't give you a loaner—
wouldn't handle right in any case, so you have to make do, laze
        about,
play solitaire on the cell phone, veg on the Red Sox, okay stuff
but not the real thing, any more than you can roll without wheels.

Not to romanticize bodies, we all know they can be a pain
in the kidneys, and they need regular servicing,
washing, and they finally wear out.

But when you get yours back, it's so good, like I said,
you just want to get in and drive away.

Marc Jampole

Impermanence

The I of me, enduring I that no one sees
behind the Facebook pose, advanced degrees,

the screaming I assaulting silent ear,
the silent I behind the thirsty tear,

the part of I that words can't mold,
that residue of I that won't be sold,

this I would never leave his sleeping mate,
her naked breasts in fall to tender flow,

areolas rising, sprawling, this I would wait
till after one more touch, and finally could not go.

This I will always dodge the falling boulder,
charging elephant, this I insists on growing older,

growing dim, taking on the I of every sign,
transforming them to other I, this anodyne

to *I'm not there*, this I that doesn't veer,
but moves through inner space to outer fear.

This I will persevere.
This I will perse
This I will pe
This I wi
This I
Th

Nancy Kerrigan

After an Evening with Poets
for Partners in Poetry

A lone light lingers in the dark living room.
The scent of Stargazer lilies permeates.
Would one have a poetry reading without flowers?
Curtains billow as if the house is breathing in and out
more peacefully than this morning. Moonlight
casts a path on the hardwood floors.

Poets gone, their words float like dust motes,
hide in corners, peek out from under chair cushions,
push out the stale air. I inhale their meanings,
tap out their meters, listen to their sounds
in the silence of midnight.

Tonight, a deceased grandfather rose again
to hike over hills. A jaundiced lover reappeared.
A jogging mother flew by, her child a hood ornament
on the stroller she pushed. The insane heard musical
pillows. The unexpected beauty of skunk cabbage
made an assertive, holy entrance.

We were all consumed by a poem of fire.

There was no dinner dish debris, no delinquent
movie rentals, yet we dined out, laughed.
We traveled out of state, out of our minds.
Ever so briefly, we too had visions, found
our own voices.

Elizabeth Kinkaid-Ehlers

Still Searching

I have spent too much of my life
thinking I should not be what I am,
not even knowing what that is.

If someone suddenly praises me,
I look around to see whom they mean,
stumbling about for a place to hide.

Caught naked in the glare of being seen,
I cloak myself in bright performance,
playing the parts that saved my life.

What would it take for me to wake
and walk through the world as who I am?

Maria Krol-Sinclair

Mean girls

Enterprises of elegance;
oh, you fistulas of fear,
how do you, slim and serpentine
at just sixteen, appear?

You'd think meanness wouldn't be so sharp in somebody so young.
But the strongest mean I ever saw
was meanness just begun.

John Krumberger

First Summer of the Trump Presidency

Something askew in the universe now:
two once in a hundred year storms
and wasps attacking without provocation.
So what good is her belief in fair play, her love of beauty,
when stung by such hatefulness she can hardly breathe?
Her tongue swells as she lurches through the garden,
trying to recall the counsel of Marcus Aurelius:
a calm mind in the face of injustice or pain.

There is a park across from the hospital.
Young men play basketball as twilight extends to evening.
It could be a painting: softening liquid sky,
athletes suspended in air, a ball bouncing against pavement
repeating the rhythm of ordinary life
as if nothing has changed.

Lesley Lambton

Consolation

For 1st Lieutenant James Garvey, and the rest of us

Your family clung to itself,
a large bear of sorrow,
so it wouldn't blow away
in the gale of its grief.

And the soldiers six
shuffled in unison,
laying hands
on one another's shoulders,
marking the distance
they would need to carry you
from the plane
to the big black car.

And in that moment,
in that silence,
a fine rain of ice dust
fell from the roof
and down onto the canopy.
It hovered a moment
above the frozen ground
then swirled and swirled itself
around our sorry bodies.

A million crystal bells ringing
that woke us from our sorrow
and made us listen.

It sounded like…
it sounded like something
you would say
if you had flown
in to save us.

Danbury Airport, Connecticut, November 28, 2014

Lesley Lambton

Observing a Family at a Poetry Reading

The father sits front row center
dressed in black
so everyone will know
he is serious and understands
the other poet
who is droning on and on
at the altar of her ego
mixing her metaphors
peacocks and asphalt
pear trees and trapdoors
oil and water
which he gladly drinks.

The mother sits with their children
further back among the people
all trapped in the heat
and their incomprehension.

One boy with wild hair
and dark, imploring eyes,
complains and wriggles and writhes.

She throws him one of those
don't-dare-do-this-to-me-now-mother-love/hate smiles
then lays his ruffled head on her lap
and strokes a simple love poem
on his back.

The whole room sighs.

Carolyn Locke

After Sky Diving

Whatever our essence is, it isn't
still. Eternally emanating outward,
colliding with others and returning
or not, maybe it flies aimlessly in one
direction after another—and so why not

leap out, let yourself be battered,
blown, and twirled? Why not tumble
head over heels and keep on going?

Stephen Hawking once said ...if we
send someone to jump into a black hole,
neither he nor his constituent atoms
will come back, but his mass energy will.
And if that applies to the whole universe,

you have to wonder
who came back from that dive,
who landed on the ground,
and what was left in the sky?

Andy Macera

The Pessimist

He already knows what will happen,
staring into the misty crystal ball of his mind.
The last shot spinning off the rim.
The winning field goal bouncing off an upright.
A grounder rolling between the first baseman's legs.
Why ask an attractive woman at a party?
She'll just deliver *no* on the grenade of a giggle,
the warhead of a loud laugh.
He's not fooled by the weatherman's patter.
Maps. Pressure. Radar.
His wand of sunshine.
There's a tornado in his tie. A hurricane in his hat.
Every numbered door conceals
a goat, a donkey, a junk car.
The wheel of fortune manipulates its momentum
until the flipper finds the black wedge of
BANKRUPT.
Most days he doesn't bother to get out of bed.
The TV on.
Children crying. Angry adults demanding answers.
They never saw it coming.
They want to scream, "This should be happening to someone else.
To you or you or you."
The stars just stare, shaking their twinkling heads.
Watching the widescreen he feels as if he is floating above.
A young boy leaning over a promenade window
on the *Hindenburg,* marveling
at the sight of Manhattan. The enormous
Empire State Building.
The world calm and smooth.
Turning quietly.
Holding a cold glass of cola like a promise,
sweaty and half-empty.

Michael Maul

Birds Who Eat French Fries

They just don't care anymore,
bellies distended,
living like bums performing
for tossed scraps
and Tater Tots
in fast food parking lots.

They were made for better things:
to float on waves,
to search for schools off shore,
or perch above the Earth
to scan for signs of prey
they once enjoyed in former days.

But junk food birds have since learned
to open crumpled bags,
and with beak and claw
to dine on human throwaways.

Pizza crusts or Taco Bell,
Mickey D's, or KFC skin and bones
locked inside of Styrofoam,
these are the tastes of sophisticated birds
who took a gigantic leap ahead.
After evolving from dinosaurs
becoming us instead.

Rennie McQuilkin

Gift

The gold and dormant koi
locked in the eye of a courtyard pool
(it reflects an oval of winter sky
from hazel to gray or vitreous blue)
are in new positions at dawn today.

They must have moved at night
like the eyes of sleepers dreaming.
It's their fins that think for them—
deeper thinking than thought.
May I too suspend my will, be realigned.

Rennie McQuilkin

Tree Smarts

for Jeff Dugan

How do trees do it?
One is leaning over Goodrich Rd.
at a 45-degree angle.
It has been doing this for eighty years.

My friend, who collects downed cedars
and anoints them with oils rubbed
into their hides, turning them to sculpture,
says trees are brainier than we think—

says they have architectural skills:
they may tilt dangerously but still
stand, thanks to the girding they install
as a way of postponing their demise.

My friend has learned from trees—
like any Redwood riven by lightning,
he has put himself together again, is all
the stronger for his joinings.

I too put off my end, lean at 45 degrees
but by God remain up right, have found
ways to hold body to soul, am not ready
for anointing. Trees give me courage.

Ilene Millman

Flowering Bamboo

Phyllostachys bambusoides last bloomed in the US in the 1960's.

There is no absolute certainty—
this is the way the world works
except when it doesn't.
Even water has no singular posture—
> rippling and embracing
> disquieting, destructive. Maybe
a God
or gods work at exception—
daring us to pare our Absolutes.

At the end of my block, a stand of bamboo—
woody, hollow stalks never budding—
for forty years never tasseling out into flower
but they will—in six or seven decades—
> gregariously—they tell me
with the certainty of time aligned.

Tiny green flowers carrying thousands of seeds
will appear some fumbled afternoon—
> forests of bamboo will burst—bloom in lockstep
in China, Japan, on my own turf.

Hope
in a future is the best I can do:
every stalk of bamboo,
every butterfly, desert pocket mouse,
and me, the pale animal
I ride—
acres of Edens tucked inside ourselves.

Naila Moreira

Sleeping in the Forest

"I thought the earth remembered me / she took me back so tenderly"
–Mary Oliver, 1935-2019

My students didn't understand
what you meant by sleeping in the forest,
my charges, so young, who nonetheless
seemed not more ageless than me.
"I think she means she died!"
squealed one at last:
the company of mists and lichen,
moisty smell of mushrooms and seeds,
too distant for the human soul alive,
too regal, too remote for us to grasp.
"Does she really?" I asked them softly
and a lively chat began:
"No, she's actually sleeping;" "No, it's a meditative
acceptance of all, a choice to forget the self— "
"No, it's a metaphor for solitude;" "for the act of poetry— "
Oh, we came up with everything,
so vigorous we felt, so young, so vibrantly one
with ourselves, nothing denied us in our strength and pride.
Yet I believed all the while that you did—you yearned
to melt into forest like a toppled tree—
inhabited by fungi, burrowed through by rabbits,
chipped at by starlight, rutted by dew,
flaking slowly away, nurse log for saplings,
fragrant with the generosity of decay.

Patricia Horn O'Brien

Time Out

A perfect drying day, sheets set a-sail in the sun
the wind endeavors to shade with strident,
indecisive clouds, the last sheet no sooner
pinned than the first lifts, dry and blank white,

above your line, beckoning you to
batten it down, along with its attendant
breeze and light, into the steady wicker
at your feet, and you lift and haul the basket

informed by all that's captured in the careless
folds of tackled flat and contoured sheets,
the blousy hills of shams, until,
at the back door, you stall before taking

the step you must back into your house's past
and all that's next. Into its more or less.

Carla Panciera

The Spoon

From the second house we've emptied out this year,
my husband sorts metal into piles—pieces of gutter,
drill bits, copper pipe. All our parents are dead now.
I have learned what I do not want to know: This
hot summer is not an aberration. It is only one
of the first. I sit on the sofa in front of the fan,
barricading myself with laundry baskets so the dog
can't get too close, cover my feet with her unthinkable fur.
My husband puts a tarnished spoon on the table before me.
Silver, he says. As if this is going to lift a curtain
like a breeze. As if, suddenly, we will walk barefoot
through the frost. This is what the spoon is to me:
another item which we must now dispose of.
This legacy of stuff that is as stultifying as August.
Cardboard shirt boxes, Belleek china, electrical cords
taped with electrical tape, body bags of t-shirts
and socks. But not, no never again, my mother
bending over a word search, or leaving footprints
of talc across the carpet after her bath.
What does my husband imagine I will do
with this spoon? How can it possibly matter? If you
were a precious metal, mined from the earth's crust,
is this what you would choose to be? I ask the spoon.
The mute spoon. This spoon with its history of polishing,
tarnishing, of assorted lips and tongues. This spoon
which reflects no light, which registers neither desire
nor regret, what is coming, what is already gone.

Garrett Phelan

Tree, Pineapple, Shoes, Fig

A year ago we were in DC
at The Women's March.
A year makes a difference.

Instead we're in Northampton
sitting at an ancestor ceremony for the passing of Ailbe,
a cousin of Denys.

I bring three sea shells and a stone to place on the altar
representing my mom, dad, sister and brother.
Who, I wonder, *is the stone?*

I heard the news that they are now
deporting undocumented Irish.

We stay the night at Richard and El's in Vermont.
Why can't we just love simply and easily?
Before bed we do simple Qi Gong with Richard.
I wonder where all my misplaced body parts are.

On the way home, down 91, I tell Jane
I'm worried about memory lapses.
She gives me four words:
Tree. Pineapple. Shoes. Fig.

Fifteen minutes later she asks
if I remember the four words.

Tree, a black birch came down in the winter storm.
Pineapples kill worms and parasites
when living in the tropics.

Victims shoes piled up and smelling
of mildew at the Holocaust Museum.

Fig tree in our yard in Virginia, but Jane
still loved to steal figs from our neighbor's tree.

We arrive home just after midnight.

Marge Piercy

Tick tock, tick shock

My knees were smashed
in an old gym when a treadmill
went crazy and threw me all
the way across the big room
past bikes, past Stairmasters
past men staring as I flew by.

For years I mourned the woods,
sand roads I had wandered, quiet
enough so I watched a fox
nibble grapes, a doe showing
something to her two fawns,
to cellar holes marked by lilacs.

But then yesterday it came
to me: if I were whole, could
still hike ten miles, the woods
would be off limits anyhow—
I'd feed thirty ticks in half
an hour now, the gift of climate

change. I've had Lyme twice,
almost croaked of babesiosis.
Young moose die from anemia.
Mice carry them everywhere.
They're armored, survive winter
and scorchers, will survive us.

Kenneth Pobo

Jerry Grew Up Thinking

that America would last forever. He
also thought that M.A.S.H. would never
go off the air. Or Carol Burnette.
Forever, like milk, has a shelf life.

He attended each July Fourth parade
carrying a little flag. In high school
his Holiday Inn boss had him
raise and lower the flag,
wrap it up nicely each dusk. Once,
on a windy day, he let it touch
the ground, prayed for forgiveness
to a God he barely believed in.
Now he wonders if America is
a drug that makes you see movie stars
and games. He remembers when

he got locked in school, lights out,
screaming for help—which did come,
but by then he could only tremble.
He's been trembling ever since.
Not showing it. Not letting his heart
touch the ground. The flag
searching for a pole where
the Holiday Inn looked
a bulldozer in the eye and lost.

Bruce Pratt

The First Cold Rain Since Spring

The first cold rain since spring,
falling in bully squalls,
carves color from the ridge,

shouts in the swollen creek,
drones in dented gutters.
The first cold rain since spring

eases in bursts of sun,
taut tongues of wild west wind,
carves color from the ridge.

Again, dark horizons
cloud autumn's equinox.
The first cold rain since spring

resumes a fierce assault
on the garden's remains,
carves color from the ridge.

The rest of the house sleeps,
burrowed as for winter as,
the first cold rain since spring
carves color from the ridge.

Geri Radacsi

Golden

50th Wedding Anniversary, September 11, 2015

Remember, we decided to choose how we'd be alone
though we would travel together?
I'd carry the egg and you'd brandish cells,

tails lashing with a thrum, blind threadlike
thousands driving to live inside my sac
though the semen that made the miracle was yours.

Remember parenthood—
milkish with suck and whining and wanting
from the child with your kick though

the child belonged to my woman's hunger
to be lifted above
the mix-up of kiss and groove and rut?

As for destiny, we'd chew it, leave it lean. That was fifty-years ago.
No, just months ago. Then we departed at the junction
of cancer, scavenging for more time.

The backpack was mine because it carried dark language
and language was mine: intubation and decompensate—
fragility.

The knock-backs were yours to bear
and evade through a slippery defense of poise,
unflinching at dumped guts of life's natural slaughter.

Higher up the mountain, breath
came in gasps. You wanted water.
I swallowed my thirst to join your body to mine.

No one but you could explore twilight's corridor
like a coyote with jagged shrieks and snapping yaps
descending sheer cliffs into rock-gulches.

None but you. I could not move,
merely hold your name, your words
given to me as shields

as you crossed an icy, golden moonlit terrain
and an owl's cry crystalized the chill.
You traveled out—as alone as I was alone.

Charles Rafferty

Candy

It was the first thing I stole. It was how I learned. Now the women in my office maintain little dishes of it beside their desks. They want me to eat it, and yet I wait until no one is looking. On my way back from the men's room, I remove what is best. I never refill. I suppress the crackling of cellophane.

Bruce Robinson

Lunar

Still yet a moon, the way it wants
to track us, mirage that never makes it,
a song, it's on the radio, miles
of quiet country, soft phrases

foundered, have my word. Tonight
rising over the risen moon and by its light
my grandmother swearing herself to sleep
I think the moon nothing but a flare

that has lonely startled us; dreams only
go so far—so fur, so feather,
her flesh and kin
scent cooler weather.

Amy Schmitz

Imago

I think of the women we were
      who wanted to fuck all day
          or at least say fuck
while we walked through cemeteries.

      Did your husband cremate you?
I don't even know
      and I was at the funeral.

I think of the women we knew
      who liked to listen or at least pretend
to listen to men in bars.
        There was always one
      with an inappropriate tattoo.

If you were alive we would wonder
      about the names.
Stanislaus seems so Slavic
      so stony.
      Why would anyone name their child that
today? There was always one with
      an accent.

I think of the women we were who said we would
      leave.
      Of all the women I knew,
    only one left.
Of all the women I knew,
      only one is left.

      If you were alive I would tell you
      about the beetle
I knocked out while sweeping the patio.
      It shimmered all day
        the way we did at parties
when we were 19 or 20.

Penelope Schott

Bless the old wheat farmers

Bless their bellies and suspenders,
the tufts of white hair in their big ears,
their kindness, in spite of their old
and politically incorrect ideas.

Let them hold open the post office door,
let them make the vestigial gesture
of half way reaching up to touch
stained bills of John Deere caps.

Let them sit together at the coffee joint,
broad shoulders not quite touching,
let them talk wheat prices or which girl
here in town had to get married,

and let them feel studly and also tender.
Who doesn't like thinking about sex,
no matter if it's been a long time?
They swallow their cooled-off coffee.

They have pushed the rock of their years
up the sloped wheat fields for a lifetime,
and that big old rock gets smoother now
even as strength goes out of their arms.

Let the rock roll down gently at the end,
not wrecking the expensive new combine.
Let the living old guys wear clean shirts
to the cemetery and study their fingernails

as they dream about seeding or harvest.

Natalie Schriefer

Late-Night Sketching

The first time I wanted to kiss someone,
I couldn't sleep, so I untangled
my earbuds and sketched. I wasn't sure
how to draw you, or me—us—
so I started with what was true:
our friend's pool, water glittering
from the spotlight and the moon,
a row of fir trees aching for the sky,
sprinkles of stars pulsating between
wisps of cloud. I drew lounge chairs;
my towel huddled in a ball; a few faceless
stick figures, our mutual friends—
and then, when I couldn't bear it any longer,
I drew what I wanted most: you,
leaning against the far wall, looking at me—
and then I drew my arms, spread wide,
as if I'd leapt off the side wall of the pool,
the sketch itself in first person,
my body almost there, suspended
in mid-air—stomach fluttering
as I waited for the drop.

Peter Shaver

In North Carolina

I'd rather spend my life
Torn between myself
And a thousand
Others

Than as a stone.

Shadowed
By Black Mountain,
I drank through a Sunday
And thought of home.

Pegi Deitz Shea

Anger Expanding

Crouching beneath the dwarf
Japanese maple, the stab
of moldy cedar mulch
behind her eyes,
the girl could still hear
anger expanding
the four walls, taste
silent tears seeping
under the closet door, feel
breaths spasm
out of the keyhole—
her mother's familiar code
of fear that fueled
her father—see
uselessness
dashing against
the windowpanes
both inside
and out.

Caroline N. Simpson

Wind Cave National Park, The Black Hills

I like to be dead
in the middle of this mystery
because here there is wind
atop peaks and whistling out a hole
that is origin to a people
who sit on my heart.

At home, there's a mess—
an imploded family
looking for carnage
without mystery or question,
not even *What happened?*

But here, wild storms
with sideways heat lightning—
pink and amber—
highlight yellow grasses for miles,
transform tall trees
into the smell of earthy needles
and vanilla cake box bark.

I belong here
with those who can read bison tails.
I walk their paths to encounter
sage white goats withstanding winds
as violent as Black Elk's pain
wailed atop the same peak.

Back home, my family members stand
on different plates across a gaping rift.
Here, I stand
with others displaced.

Once below ground,
the earth cracked open— an eggshell.
From small hole, a people anew
sowed in long stretches of yellow,

how the highlights in my hair
pulled me out of a winter,
my skin bronze and warm
as rock rising from plains
to the bluest of skies,

muting any suburban blue
far far away.

Here, my eyes pierce the horizon—
so easy to break into
land and sky—
that I may step between,
a space for myself
on this earth.

John Stanizzi

Bones as Feathers

> *O yes, our lives are going on without us.*
> *O no, we never finish chasing.*
> —James Tate, Hidden Drives

James Tate and I were dear friends, though we never met.
I called on his wisdom when the two lovers met.

The landscape would grow more strange as the weather cooled.
Remember November's kiss; lips shivering, met.

The city was charming and the years passed as air.
We would sit on the hill where sky and river met.

Were we so blind we couldn't see the snow or rain?
Were we deaf—couldn't hear when fear and weather met?

Father of a small city, my back is aching,
even now, when morning denies endeavors met.

My bones have become feathers; they're the weight of light,
and from shade one comes to harvest all pleasure met.

James would joke that our lives will go on without us.
Don't ever pretend, John, that you two never met.

Susan Finch Stevens

The Idea of Grief at Key West

*on learning of the death of Mary Oliver while at Key West
attending a poetry workshop about animals*

How else to grieve her death of voice
than to attend through this car window
the osprey flying low along my course
as though an escort as my mind recalls
the maker of the song she sang the world
of the world as footing for us all?

In bearing stalks of grass to line its nest,
this osprey bears not a rosary of grief
but of hope that streams behind it
in its task that will continue, noted or not.
It is the noting that my task becomes,
and in the noting, that she and I
and grief and hope and this osprey are one.

Steve Straight

Old Longtooth

for the Hill-Stead Museum, Farmington, Connecticut

During a drought in 1913 the Italian workmen,
struggling to dig a water trench on the grounds
of the great estate, kept stubbing their shovels
on thick roots of something well below
the waterlogged turf, until one of them
stopped and called out, "Non radice, ossa, ossa!"

And sure enough, as they felt their way
with their fingers now, down through the sticky clay,
they did find bones, heavy and ancient,
what the professor called in from Yale
would confirm was *Mammut americanum*,
the American mastodon.

It's not hard to imagine this stocky elephant of old
standing in the late Pleistocene winter,
his shaggy brown coat dusted with snow
as the flexible trunk grabs twigs and
branches from the lark, spruce, and pine
in the Hill-Stead hills fifteen thousand years ago
as the glaciers retreat to the north.

There are no buildings, of course, no buildings at all,
and the very occasional neighbors are the dire wolf,
the short-faced bear, a beaver of three hundred pounds,
or the giant ground sloth lumbering by in the forest.

Nine feet at the shoulder, with curved tusks just as long,
he was a solitary being, browsing his fill
a full-time job at a weight of five tons,
cracking off limbs with his tusks and
grinding them down with his nipple-shaped molars.

At death there was "no sign of foul play,"
as the professor said, no proof of Clovis hunters
taking him down, just a few thousand years
from extinction, anyway, having roamed the earth
for a million. Tuberculosis may have claimed him.

If one were still around, as Jefferson had hoped,
no doubt it would be chained somewhere, trotted out
for show under threat of the bullhook, a spectacle
in a world that seems to feed on celebrity.

Whatever drew you to this swampy depression,
moss or pine cones or just a drink of pure water,
I for one am glad you are not here today
to see this circus, this three-ring earth.

Tim Suermondt

The Night Sea, Quiet, in Provincetown

Lights in the distance—
pin pricks really—are all
that can be seen.
In your imagination, pirate ships
and lost sailors
who won't ever be disembarking
appear and disappear.
Birds are flying, but you can't
see them—you close
the door of your bungalow, go
to bed and dream
of saturating light, and sandpipers
shuttling with pomp
across the beach sand like kings.

Nancy Swanson

Small Change

In the back seat of our rented Mustang Convertible,
looking even smaller than 86 pounds,
she huddles into her white sweater,
a Christmas gift the year Ronald Reagan was elected.

My sister smiles at me from the driver's seat,
celebrating the bribe that pried Mama,
surrounded by relics of a lifetime,
from the recliner with a view of the asphalt parking lot.

She has no memory of 52 years with Daddy,
seven grandchildren, our husbands and names,
or her 60-year love affair with Lucky Strikes,
a relief to caretakers who push patients to the smoking garden.

But the offer of a beer from two middle-aged women
with familiar faces tucked her behind me, shivering
in the eighty-degree Florida breeze, reading signs:
Stop, McDonald's, Whiskey Creek Road, Four Miles to Ft. Myers.

Having looked at the morning paper, solved the jumble
and dropped it in her lap, she is happy to sip Budweiser
between crumbling front teeth she insists don't hurt
and talk about the sister she hasn't spoken to for sixty years.

And her beloved father, whose heart broke with the Depression.
We do know her, the four-year-old who taught herself to read,
graduated at 15, won every card game she ever played,
there, underneath the tarnish, as bright as a new, 1918 penny.

Aidan VanSuetendael

August Partum

On mornings when only a thin film of sweat
separated our bodies,
when humid air left a haze on the blue mirror,

the next-door dogs caroled us awake
and we were waterborn into the day,
gently into the late summer.

In the mornings when ringing of nails on coffee cups
breached the curtained quiet,
when sunlight shone in dust kaleidoscope beams,

it was as if we were the first to feel the sun,
as if we were delivered into late summer slowly,
from darkness into ochre August Sunday.

Lee Varon

Kindergarten

for my son in detox

Your first day of kindergarten:
in your sweater vest,
clutching your dinosaur lunchbox,
smile wide.
Who was to know what lay ahead
as the Tyrannosaurus and Triceratops
took over your life
ravenous, unforgiving,
and me—
clutching my camera,
trembling at the world you were about to enter.

Andrew Vogel

Passage

Once Kimmy was old enough to escort
herself to her little friends' houses,
Mom was so fed up with the slamming
gate she made Dad take it down,
and the walkway from the back porch
that ran between the firm, vertical posts
opened onto the alleyway and freedom itself.

Baby sister of three tough brothers,
Kimmy could take off; she could run,
choose, go anywhere, do anything,
pound the whole damn world down
under the slick soles of her Converse,

but the years gathered on her legs,
and her folks needed her more then
more as Dad's spine slowly decomposed
and the checks started to peter out.

The boys all broke themselves loose
with jobs, and wives, and booze,
but she's there with Mom still,
the mortgage now her sole possession.

She remembers the vacation they took.
The shore. The starfish she found
and named, and tried to teach to live
in a bucket of salted water on the porch
of their rental three blocks from the beach.
The next day it was gone.
Before they left she found it,
dried hard in the roadside gravel
half way back to the flare of the ocean waves.

She remembers the cree and slam
that chased her pace down the alley.
Now the ruined gray posts sag with the fence,
dilapidated as an old fighter's mouth,
and every day Kim hustles down
the walk and through that long-silent gate
with nowhere really to carry herself.

R. Bratten Weiss

In the Garden

That feeling you get when you just swallowed a ghost.
It is by accident.
You are out in the garden eating tiny cherry tomatoes
ripe from the vine, eating them very quickly.
Because it is September, and time is sloping away.
The tomatoes are red like gems or poison.
You don't notice until suddenly there is another
something inside of you, and it is grieving,
because it can never eat tomatoes in September again,
or touch the bodies that it loved, or even take a proper shit.
O, let me stay, let me stay a while it says,
knocking against your skull like Catherine rapping
on Heathcliff's window in the storm.
You feel so sad for it, the lost thing.
Then you realize you never swallowed a ghost at all
and it was just you all along.

Will Wells

First Temptation to Resist

My father teaches me how to sharpen
sticks against rough sidewalks. Hardship hardened,
he passes on slum lore to his pampered son.

A high, barbed, chain-link fence still defends
tennis club courts from poor boys wanting in,
but, just outside, revived temptation bends

its limbs—a crab-apple tree, laden again
with bitter fruit that no one wants to own.
So unpicked apples drop off to wizen

and rot into an alternate fortune,
spitted on sticks, perfectly putrid and round,
lobbed high to maximize their splatter zone—

Molotov fruit cocktails in the fenced compound.
My father stoops to reload our weapons,
and we serve together, sharing his wounds.

John Sibley Williams

Counterglow

Consider the meteorite,
        110,000 pounds of

debris that hollowed out
        Wolfe Creek Crater;

how Oppenheimer's boldest
        nightmares couldn't

concoct the kind of ruin
        that vanishes a sky

for years; how anything can
        become a tourist attraction.

Consider what we do to ourselves
        when the one person we love

renounces our touch. Consider angels,
        my grandmother used to say,

& how you never know which saves
        & which consumes us; whatever

you believe, how it all comes down
        to flame. There's too much

written about the end. Pale horses &
        rogue nukes & the smaller gods

of razor & lukewarm bathwater. When I
        consider each meal is someone's

last, am I meant to lose my appetite
        or keep dragging my fork

over this emptied plate, never sated?
        Consider how we become our own

conclusion; how what we've hung out
        to dry remains crucified; how believing

these things beautiful might not make them so.
        Consider how rivers multiply

into ocean; a few misplaced words & now
        the bombs have their wings.

& so much goddamn waiting, as if we have to
        imagine what nooses do to necks.

Consider what's been redacted from life
        to make all this anguish seem an art.

Martin Willitts Jr.

The Summer When I Was Seven

Hundreds of millers hovered
and smashed against the porch light.
Those moths lodged and struggled to get free
of the mesh screen door,
their white wings beating frantically.

After playing war all day, shooting cap guns,
no one wanted to come in,
although our mothers did roll-call.
The night was perfect for last acts.
Soon, we'd have to slog to school again.
We'd have to answer to questions.
If you asked, *What did you do all summer?*
we'd probably say, *Nothing.*

You can pack a lot of stupidity in three months.
I killed my share of minutes. I'd spin in circles,
get as dizzy as the millers. I slammed the screen door
going in and out of chores, mostly avoiding them,
until they stacked up and I got into more trouble
than I could avoid. If you asked me, I'd say
I was stir-crazy, ready to burst out of my skin.
If I could have swarmed into the bright lights,
I'd probably would, just to know how it felt
to live like that.

I don't know what drove me. I'm too old
to remember why I wanted to crash and burn,
why war was so fascinating. I guess it was because
war wasn't tangible at seven.
My dad never talked about it. I almost wish he had.
I'd get an idea of the senselessness.
I'd dive for cover. I wouldn't end up in Vietnam
finding out the hard way.

CONNECTICUT POETRY SOCIETY
PRIZE WINNERS

Connecticut Poetry Award, 2018
Judge: Daniel Donaghy

1st Prize
Clemonce Heard
"Neighbors"

2nd Prize
Pat Hale
"An Oak Leaf in the Shape of an Owl"

3rd Prize
Judith Nacca
"The Last Word"

About the Judge: Daniel Donaghy is the author of the poetry collections *Somerset* (NYQ Books, 2018), *Start with the Trouble* (University of Arkansas Press, 2009), and *Streetfighting* (BkMk Press, 2005). Raised in Philadelphia, he is now Professor of English at Eastern Connecticut State University, where he received the Board of Regents Teaching Award and the CSU Norton Mezvinsky Trustees Research Award. He is currently the Poet Laureate of Windham, Connecticut.

Clemonce Heard
First Prize, *Connecticut Poetry Award, 2018*

Neighbors
Stillwater, OK

How long did it take to paint the flag
on the ga / rage's back wall is not what I asked

myself or my live-in-lover, backing out of
the driveway, heading back to where we'd

just turned, looking for a place to stay.
We were greeted by a law / n of trucks & cars,

Hot Wheels that had grown & greyed,
& the Confederate mural for us to marvel.

It couldn't have been that diffi / cult; Seeing
as the design is rather simple: A diademed 'X'

of thirteen stars, an intersection of dreams
& the red that surrounds it: The red necks,

the red trucks, the red text, the red rust
all pointing to the odd of it all. A single man

could've pulled it off. Could've brushed,
or rather slathered pain / t from canister

to wall, but two stories means family,
so I picture a wife drafting the southern cross,

& kids filling the s / tars. Say, can you see
an open garage aerating the latex exhaust?

Neighbors walking t / heir children, pointing
past the mower, shovels, ladders & saws?

Racism takes teamwork, takes the anointment
of offspring. I can almost see their gawking

once the wall was finished. The man kissing
his wife's temple, both with one arm around

each other & the other around their kids.
Or the image could've existed in the house

when they moved in, a photo whistling
"welcome niggers" they'd failed to take down.

Pat Hale
Second Prize, Connecticut Poetry Award, 2018

An Oak Leaf in the Shape of an Owl

Sometimes a leaf leaves its branch
but doesn't find the ground. It gets caught
in flight to become a question, an illusion,

a shape that draws someone closer
to a window. Becomes a shadow,
brittle in its browning, a reconstruction

of something green. Familiar,
like writing on an envelope whose letter
has been lost, contents forgotten,

but the hand that moved across the paper
still known, undeniable. The same hand
that held the pen and shuffled cards

laid out games of solitaire again and again,
red on black on red until the cards went soft
with use and time. Hearts and diamonds

collected into piles, tapped straight,
and set aside, to be gathered up
when the game was over.

The presence of absence is not the same
as grief. My old gray cat lies in the yard,
beneath the tulips bulbs that bloom in Spring.

My mother lies beneath her stone,
dates cleanly carved and surface shining.

Judith Nacca
Third Prize, Connecticut Poetry Award, 2018

The Last Word

A voicemail from my mother
six years after her death,
pressed like a wildflower
between psalms.

The first year,
I listened daily.
The sound of her voice
both filled and emptied,
like a cold wind ever-passing
through the hole
blown through everything.

Now, I save it for days
when her absence
is so palpable, it holds me
with my own arms.

And for moments
I believe her words,
even as they scatter
their impossible physics
all over the room:

*I'm running late. Be there
in twenty minutes.*

Though I know better,
I let myself look out the window.
Forehead flat against the pane.
Hands cupping each side of my gaze;
intentional parentheses.

Connecticut River Review Poetry Prize, 2018
Judge: Daniel Donaghy

1st Prize
Robert Claps
"Jump Shots at Sixty"

2nd Prize
Lynn McGee
"Time Rises Like a Flood"

3rd Prize
Linda Haviland Conte
"A Last Visit"

About the Judge: Daniel Donaghy is the author of the poetry collections *Somerset* (NYQ Books, 2018), *Start with the Trouble* (University of Arkansas Press, 2009), and *Streetfighting* (BkMk Press, 2005). Raised in Philadelphia, he is now Professor of English at Eastern Connecticut State University, where he received the Board of Regents Teaching Award and the CSU Norton Mezvinsky Trustees Research Award. He is currently the Poet Laureate of Windham, Connecticut.

Robert Claps
First Prize, Connecticut River Review *Poetry Prize, 2018*

Jump Shots at Sixty

I could take a ride down Route 5 again, pull up to the rims rusting
 between the Catholic church and the train tracks,
I could ignore the fleeting back pain and dismiss my doctor's good
 advice
by dribbling down the length of the court, dodging the broken glass
 and chunks of asphalt,
and stopping just inside what's left of the foul line for a jump shot, a
 little mid-range one
that I will take for my father, for his wavy black hair slicked back and
 shining, and that tipsy Dean Martin weave he did at
 weddings,
crooning "Send Me A Pillow To Cry On" to all the women,
and maybe a shot off the backboard for the day he took me and my
 first love to the state fair with the side money he made fixing
 cracked engine blocks,
and here, at the wing, a fade-away for his first-born infant's grave,
 and his brother's three rows down,
and a baseline shot for the blessed plastic statue he kept on the
 dashboard of his '62 Chrysler New Yorker, a miniature Jesus
 that couldn't save him from the Thorazine and dozens of
 electric shocks at the West Haven V.A.,
and how about a Dave Cowens shot, that half-hook, half-jumper, for
 the million Camels and the nips of Seagram's despite the
 strokes and the amputated toes,
and a Hail Mary for the black-and-white of him waving from a troop
 train leaving for Quantico, 1943, his eyes cast down as if
 looking for a sign, the way his eyes looked down at the
 waxed floor when I left him yesterday, gripping his walker in
 a room he shares with strangers,
for that photo I keep on my desk, a final lob from three-point land,
my right elbow tucked in tight, making the ball arc so high
I can whisper a prayer
in the moments before it falls back to earth.

Lynn McGee
Second Prize, Connecticut River Review *Poetry Prize, 2018*

Time Rises Like a Flood

It's isn't the loss of you I resist,
but the forgetting,
reaching into dark water and finding
nothing. Rain drums
against the eaves, but April
was effusive and sunny
when you died. Your daughter
sat cross-legged on the floor
of a waiting room, pushing cars
across the carpet.
Your sons passed a Gameboy
back and forth, divers sharing
air. Your children
completed themselves,
without you. I see your wary
intelligence in their lean
faces. I'm willing myself
to hear you clear your throat,
to watch you rub lotion,
absent-mindedly,
up the backs of your arms.
I inhabit your memory,
lace my feet into your boots,
put my hands
on the steering wheel where
your hands warmed it—
but that sense of you lingering,
is gone. That panic
that you're lost, somewhere,
is gone. Water rises
between us, weaving
its layers.

Linda Haviland Conte
Third Prize, Connecticut River Review *Poetry Prize, 2018*

A Last Visit

He gamely tries to dandle my son,
his grandson, on his knee,
knowing I'd want that,
to see them together—
though next time we know
he won't be strong enough
and I won't bring my son.

He tries to tell me some story
from when he was young.
He knows I like those
and he produces a photo taken out
in preparation for our visit.
It must have been one of the first
cars his family ever owned,
a Model A Tudor Sedan, but
the people in the photo weren't
anyone I'd have known.

A one-time Lieutenant Colonel
setting traps for Hitler's forces
he quietly declares he's tired,
and makes his way to bed while
Mom and I hover behind
lest he should fall.

Winners of CPS contests are not eligible to win any CPS contest the following year.

CONNECTICUT POETRY SOCIETY CONTESTS

CONNECTICUT POETRY AWARD

In honor of Connecticut Poetry Society founders,
Wallace Winchell, Ben Brodine, and Joseph Brodinsky

Made possible through the generous support of
The Adolf and Virginia Dehn Foundation

Open to all poets
Opens: April 1
Deadline: May 31
Fee $15 for up to 3 unpublished poems, any form, 80-line limit
Prizes: 1st – $400; 2nd – $100; 3rd – $50

Winning poems will be published in *Connecticut River Review* and
posted on the Connecticut Poetry Society website.

Winners receive a free, two-year membership in the Connecticut
Poetry Society. Simultaneous submissions are acceptable; however,
please notify us immediately upon acceptance elsewhere.

Electronic Submissions Only
Submit at: www.connecticutriverreview.submittable.com.

Submit up to three previously unpublished poems, in one document,
no more than one poem per page; 80-line limit. No contact info
on poems (contact information will be requested separately via
Submittable).

Guidelines are available on the CPS website: www.ctpoetry.net

CONNECTICUT RIVER REVIEW POETRY CONTEST

made possible through the generosity of the Connecticut Poetry Society

Open to all poets
Opens: August 1
Deadline: September 30
Fee $15 for up to 3 unpublished poems, any form, 80-line limit
Prizes: 1st – $400; 2nd – $100; 3rd – $50

Winning poems will be published in *Connecticut River Review* and posted on the Connecticut Poetry Society website.

Winners receive a free, two-year membership in the Connecticut Poetry Society. Simultaneous submissions are acceptable; however, please notify us immediately upon acceptance elsewhere.

Electronic Submissions Only
Submit at: www.connecticutriverreview.submittable.com.

Submit up to three previously unpublished poems, in one document, no more than one poem per page; 80-line limit. No contact info on poems (contact information will be requested separately via Submittable).

Guidelines are available on the CPS website: www.ctpoetry.net

NUTMEG POETRY AWARD

made possible through the generosity of the Connecticut Poetry Society

Open to Connecticut poets only
Opens: December 1
Deadline: January 31
Fee: Members of CPS may enter this contest without paying a fee; for non-members the fee is $10.
Prizes: 1st – $200; 2nd – $100; 3rd – $50

Winning poems will be posted on the Connecticut Poetry Society website.

Winners receive a free, two-year membership in the Connecticut Poetry Society. Simultaneous submissions are acceptable; however, please notify us immediately upon acceptance elsewhere.

Electronic Submissions Only
Submit at: www.connecticutriverreview.submittable.com.

Submit up to three previously unpublished poems, in one document, no more than one poem per page; 80-line limit. No contact info on poems (contact information will be requested separately via Submittable).

Guidelines are available on the CPS website: www.ctpoetry.net

LYNN DECARO POETRY COMPETITION

In memory of Lynn DeCaro, a promising young Connecticut Poetry Society member who died of leukemia in 1986

Made possible through the generous support of
The Betty and Allen DeCaro Family

Open to Connecticut student poets in grades 9-12
Opens: January 1
Deadline: March 15
Prizes: 1st – $75; 2nd – $50; 3rd – $25
No fee for up to 3 unpublished poems, 40-line limit

Winning poems will be posted on the Connecticut Poetry Society website.

Winners receive a free, two-year membership in the Connecticut Poetry Society. Simultaneous submissions are acceptable; however, please notify us immediately upon acceptance elsewhere.

Electronic Submissions Only
Submit at: www.connecticutriverreview.submittable.com.

Submit up to three previously unpublished poems, in one document, no more than one poem per page; 80-line limit. No contact info on poems (contact information will be requested separately via Submittable).

Guidelines are available on the CPS website: www.ctpoetry.net

CONTRIBUTOR NOTES

Connecticut River Review
extends its sincere appreciation
to all its contributors.

Chris Abbate's poems have appeared in numerous journals. He has been nominated for the Pushcart Prize and a Best of the Net award, and has received awards in the Nazim Hikmet Poetry Competition and the North Carolina Poetry Society's Thomas H. McDill contest. Abbate's first book of poetry, *Talk About God*, was published by Main Street Rag in September 2017. Originally from Wethersfield, Connecticut, Abbate now resides in Apex, North Carolina. (chrisabbate.com)

Laura Altshul, a retired educator, tutors and serves on non-profit boards focused on providing educational and arts experiences for New Haven's children whose families don't ordinarily have access to these opportunities. Her two books of poetry are *Searching for the Northern Lights* and *Bodies Passing*. She had her husband Victor Altshul co-lead the New Haven Chapter of the Connecticut Poetry Society.

Carol Amato is a natural science educator and author of a nature series (ten books) published by Barron's Educational Series, Inc. and John Wiley & Sons (*Backyard Pets: Exploring Nature Close to Home*). She conducts classroom natural science programs to encourage inquiry and conservation awareness in young children. Amato's poetry has appeared in many journals and anthologies, and she has received a Pushcart nomination.

Sherri (Sheryll) Bedingfield's poetry has been published in several anthologies and small press publications. She has presented her poetry at many Connecticut venues and has read her poetry in Dingle, Ireland. Several of Bedingfield's poems have been performed by East Haddam Stage Company. She is the author of two books of poetry: *Transitions and Transformations* (2010) and *The Clattering, Voices from Old Forfarshire, Scotland* (2016). Bedingfield is a psychotherapist and a family therapist.

Ace Boggess is author of four books of poetry, most recently *I Have Lost the Art of Dreaming It So* (Unsolicited Press, 2018) and *Ultra Deep Field* (Brick Road Poetry Press, 2017), and the novel *A Song Without a Melody* (Hyperborea Publishing, 2016). His writing has appeared in many literary journals. He received a fellowship from the West

Virginia Commission on the Arts and spent five years in a West Virginia prison. He lives in Charleston, West Virginia.

Daniel Bourne's books include *The Household Gods* (Cleveland State) and *Where No One Spoke the Language* (CustomWords). The recipient of four Ohio Arts Council poetry fellowships, he teaches at The College of Wooster in NE Ohio, where he edits *Artful Dodge*. He has spent quite a lot of time in Poland. Bourne's bilingual collaborative poetry project "A Journey Between the Lands" with Tadeusz Dziewanowski was featured in the January 2015 issue of *Plume*, and his poetry/visual art collaboration with Wojciech Kołyszko, "A Deep Map of Sobieszewo Island," appeared on the *Portland Review*'s website. Bourne's translations of Polish political poet Tomasz Jastrun are also in Penguin's anthology of Eastern European poetry, *Child of Europe* and in Norton's *Against Forgetting: Twentieth-Century Poetry of Witness*. Salmon Run Press published a book of his translations of Jastrun's poetry and essays, *On the Crossroads of Asia and Europe*. He's published a number of translations of other Polish poets as well.

Roxana L. Cazan is an Assistant Professor of English at Saint Francis University in Pennsylvania, where she teaches World and Postcolonial Literature and Creative Writing. She is a translator of Romanian. Her translation of Matei Vişniec's "Teeth" was nominated for a Pushcart Prize by Reunion, at UT Dallas. Her poems have been featured in numerous journals and anthologies. Cazan's full-length poetry book, *The Accident of Birth*, was published by Main Street Rag in 2017.

Robert Claps lives with his wife and a few dogs in eastern Connecticut. He is retired from a career in information technology. Recent work is forthcoming or has appeared in *2 Bridges, Margie: An American Journal of Poetry, Crab Creek Review*, and other journals. Claps could be assembling a book-length manuscript for publication, but he'd rather just concentrate on writing the next poem.

Lauren Coggins lives in South Carolina and works in the insurance industry. Her poems have appeared previously in *Southern Poetry Review, Reed Magazine*, and *Jabberwock* and she has work forthcoming in *The Briar Cliff Review*.

Linda Haviland Conte is the author of *Slow as a Poem* (Ibbetson Street Press, 2002). Her poems are included in the anthologies *City of Poets: 18 Boston Voices* and *Out of the Blue Writers Unite*. She is Treasurer of the New England Poetry Club, and has participated as a panelist at the Massachusetts and New Hampshire Poetry Festivals (2017). Conte won a Cambridge Poetry Award for Best Short Poem. A graduate of Connecticut College, she was a founding member and occasional editor for *Ibbetson Street* magazine in its early years.

Ken Craft is a University of Connecticut graduate now living west of Boston. His poems have appeared in *The Writer's Almanac*, *Verse Daily*, *Plainsong*, and numerous other journals and e-zines. He is the author of two collections of poetry, *Lost Sherpa of Happiness* (Kelsay Books, 2017) and *The Indifferent World* (Future Cycle Press, 2016).

Barbara Crooker is a poetry editor for *Italian Americana*, and author of nine full-length books of poetry; *Some Glad Morning* is forthcoming in the Pitt Poetry Series. Her awards include the WB Yeats Society of New York Award, the Thomas Merton Poetry of the Sacred Award, and three Pennsylvania Council on the Arts Creative Writing Fellowships. Her work appears in a variety of anthologies, including *Common Wealth: Contemporary Poets on Pennsylvania*, and *The Bedford Introduction to Literature*.

Kika Dorsey's work has been published in numerous journals and books. She has published a poetry chapbook, *Beside Herself* (Flutter Press, 2010) and two full-length collections, *Rust* and *Coming Up for Air*. (Word Tech Editions, 2016, 2018). Dorsey has a Ph.D. in Comparative Literature from the University of Washington in Seattle. She lives in Boulder, Colorado, and enjoys running and hiking in the mountains and plains of her Colorado home.

Anna Elkins is a traveling poet and painter. She earned a BA in art and English and an MFA and Fulbright Fellowship in poetry. Elkins has written, painted, and taught on six continents. Her art hangs on walls around the world, and she has published four books, including the poetry chapbook, *The Space Between*. (www.annaelkins.com)

Chris Espenshade, an archaeologist, branched into creative writing in 2017. He's had more than 30 works accepted for publication, most recently in *The Raven Chronicle's Journal*, *The Dead Mule School of Southern Literature*, and *Fewer Than 500*. Espenshade lives in Wellsboro, Pennsylvania.

O.A. Fraser was born in Guyana, South America. Fraser matriculated to the University of Chicago, and continues to call its neighborhood, Hyde Park, home. His work has appeared in numerous publications. He is a member of The Perspectivists, one of the longest continuously existing writers' groups in Chicago. Past participants include Pulitzer winner Gwendolyn Brooks, and Sam Greenlee of *The Spook Who Sat by the Door* fame. Fraser also hosts Shape Note (Fasola) singings in his home once a month.

Jennifer L. Freed lives with her husband and two teenage daughters in Massachusetts. Recent work appears or is forthcoming in *Atlanta Review*, *Zone 3*, and *Worcester Review*. A chapbook, *These Hands Still Holding* (Finishing Line Press), was a finalist in the 2013 New Women's Voices contest.

Margaret Gibson, the current Connecticut Poet Laureate, is the author of twelve books of poems, all from LSU Press, most recently *Not Hearing the Wood Thrush*, 2018. A poem from that collection, "Passage" was included in *The Best American Poetry*, 2017.

Gary Glauber is a poet, fiction writer, teacher, and former music journalist. His works have received multiple Pushcart Prize and Best of the Net nominations. He champions the underdog to the melodic rhythms of obscure power pop. He has published two collections, *Small Consolations* (Aldrich Press) and *Worth the Candle* (Five Oaks Press), and a chapbook, *Memory Marries Desire* (Finishing Line Press).

Carol Grametbauer is the author of two chapbooks, *Homeplace* (Main Street Rag, 2018) and *Now & Then* (Finishing Line Press, 2014). Her poems have appeared in journals including *Appalachian Heritage*, *The Sow's Ear Poetry Review*, and *Pine Mountain Sand & Gravel*, as well as in a number of anthologies.

Connie Jordan Green writes a newspaper column, poetry, and young people's novels (*The War at Home and Emmy*). She has two chapbooks, *Slow Children Playing* and *Regret Comes to Tea*, from Finishing Line Press, a collection, *Household Inventory*, winner of the Brick Road Poetry Press Award, and, most recently, *Darwin's Breath*, from Iris Press. Her poetry has appeared in numerous journals and anthologies. She teaches writing for various groups. She lives with her husband and several cats and dogs on a farm in Loudon County, Tennessee. They have three children and seven grandchildren.

William Greenway's Selected Poems was the Poetry Book of the Year Award winner from FutureCycle Press, and his tenth collection, *Everywhere at Once,* won the Poetry Book of the Year Award from the Ohio Library Association, as did his eighth collection *Ascending Order*. Greenway won the Helen and Laura Krout Memorial Poetry Award, the Larry Levis Editors' Prize from *Missouri Review,* the Open Voice Poetry Award from *The Writer's Voice,* the State Street Press Chapbook Competition, an Ohio Arts Council Grant, an Academy of American Poets Prize, and he been named Georgia Author of the Year. Greenway is Distinguished Professor of English Emeritus at Youngstown State University, and now lives in Ephrata, PA, where he teaches at Lebanon Valley College.

Pat Hale is the author of the poetry collection, *Seeing Them with My Eyes Closed,* and the chapbook, *Composition and Flight*. Her work appears in many journals and anthologies, and has been awarded CALYX's Lois Cranston Memorial Poetry Prize, the Sunken Garden Poetry Prize, and first prize in the Al Savard Poetry Competition. She lives in West Hartford, Connecticut and serves on the board of directors for the Riverwood Poetry Series. She is particularly fond of ekphrastic poetry.

A. Hampford is a writer, traveler, yogi, lover of nature and animals (especially dogs). Currently, she is working on a chapbook inspired by a trip to Antarctica and the aging process. She is based in Connecticut but spends time on the coast of Ecuador, enjoying life in another language.

Clemonce Heard is the 2019-2020 Ronald Wallace Poetry Fellow. His work has appeared in *Obsidian, Ruminate, The Missouri Review,* and *World Literature Today,* and other publications. He was awarded an honorable mention in the 2017 Gwendolyn Brooks Centennial Poetry Prize, a runner-up for the 2018 Tennessee Williams Literary Festival Poetry Award, 2nd place in the 2018 Janet B. McCabe Poetry Prize, and was a finalist in the 2019 Jeffrey E. Smith Editor's Prize. He is a New Orleans native and current Tulsa Artist Fellow.

Max Heinegg is a singer-songwriter and recording artist whose records can be heard at www.maxheinegg.com. He lives and teaches English in the public schools of Medford, Massachusetts. Heinegg's poems have been nominated for Best of the Net and The Pushcart Prize. His poems have appeared in many literary journals.

Jenna Heller grew up in Connecticut, lived in Texas for seven years, and now lives in New Zealand with her partner, their two teens, two cats, and a dog. More of her writing can be found in *Star 82 Review, Takahē,* and *The Wax Paper.*

Paul Hostovsky is the author of ten books of poetry, most recently, *Late for the Gratitude Meeting* (Kelsay Books, 2019). His poems have won a Pushcart Prize, two Best of the Net awards, and have been featured on *Poetry Daily, Verse Daily,* and *The Writer's Almanac.* (paulhostovsky.com)

Tony Howarth a playwright, director, former journalist, retired in 1991 after 28 years as a high school teacher of English and theatre at Woodlands High School in Westchester, NY. He began writing poetry in 2009 after a visit to William Wordsworth's Dove Cottage, in England's Lake District. Much of his poetry focuses on the pleasures and perplexities of growing old.

Jenevieve Carlyn Hughes is a graduate student who writes about spirituality and contemplative ecology. She currently resides in Connecticut.

David Hummon is a poet, painter, and professor emeritus of Holy Cross College in Worcester, Massachusetts. As well as poetry for adults, he has published an award-winning book of children's poetry,

Animal Acrostics (Dawn Publications, 1999).

Marc Jampole wrote *Music from Words* (Bellday Books, 2007) and *Cubist States of Mind / Not the Cruelest Month* (Poet's Haven Press, 2017). His poetry has appeared in many journals and anthologies. Approximately 1,800 freelance articles he has written have been published. A former television reporter and public relations executive, Jampole writes the OpEdge blog, which appears on the websites of three national publications. He is president of the board of *Jewish Currents*, a national magazine of politics and arts.

Nancy Kerrigan is the author of two chapbooks: *The Poetry of Psychiatry* and *High Heels & Sneakers*. Her book *Lucky Enough, A Journey* is forthcoming. Many of the poems in this collection convey the process of looking back and reflecting.

Elizabeth Kinkaid-Ehlers moved to Connecticut in 1979 for a one-year appointment as Visiting Writer in Residence at Trinity College. She liked living here so much that she retrained and stayed on as a private practice psychotherapist. Three of her sons and their families live in Connecticut, giving her wonderful times with their families. According to family legend, she began making poems when she was three years old, engaging her mother as amanuensis. She won a Hopwood Award in Poetry as an undergraduate at the University of Michigan. *Leaping and Looming* was published in 2005, *Seasoning* in 2009 and *How Do I Hate Thee: A Sampler of Poetic Rage Against Cancer* in 2011.

Maria Krol-Sinclair is a writer of prose and poetry living in Washington DC. She holds a BA in Modern Languages from Pitzer College.

John Krumberger's work has been published in numerous literary journals. Backwaters Press published his first full-length volume of poetry entitled *The Language of Rain and Wind*. His latest volume of poems, *Because Autumn*, was published in 2016 by Main Street Rag Press. He lives with his wife in Minneapolis and works as a psychologist in private practice in St. Paul.

Lesley Lambton was born in Newcastle-upon-Tyne, England—a city famous for its coal and Brown Ale. After gaining a degree in English Literature, she moved to Cardiff in Wales, where she joined the Collective Writers. There she had several of her poems published in anthologies including *Of Sawn Grain and Private People – Self Portraits in Verse*. In 1996, with support from the Welsh Arts Council, the Collective Press published her chapbook *Crocus*. She now lives in Ridgefield, Connecticut, where she works in her dream job at her local library organizing programs and events.

Carolyn Locke is the author of three poetry collections: *Always This Falling* (2010), *The Place We Become* (2015), and *The Riddle of Yes* (2019)— and a haibun entitled *Not One Thing: Following Matsuo Basho's Narrow Road to the Interior* (2013) that weaves prose, haiku, and photographs in a meditative exploration of her 2009 travels in Japan. A graduate of Bates College and the MFA in Creative Writing Program at Goddard College, Locke taught high school English, creative writing, and humanities classes for many years and was the recipient of teacher travel grants to Japan, Morocco, and China. She and her husband currently live in Troy, Maine.

Andy Macera is the recipient of awards from *Plainsongs, Mad Poets Review*, and *Philadelphia Poets*. His work has also appeared in many other journals. He lives in West Chester, Pennsylvania.

Michael Maul lives on Florida's Gulf Coast. His poems have appeared in literary journals and anthologies in and outside the U.S. For two consecutive years his submissions for the Ireland-based FISH Publishing's poetry anthology contest were longlisted. Maul is also a past winner of the Mercantile Library Prize for Fiction, and in 2018 he authored *Dancing Naked in Front of Dogs*, a full-length collection of poetry. One of his works, "Anniversary Poem", was included in a year-end recap of her top twelve favorite poems of 2018, compiled by widely followed poetry blogger Charlotte Hamrick (Zouxzoux).

Lynn McGee is the author of the poetry collections *Tracks* (Broadstone Books, 2019); *Sober Cooking* (Spuyten Duyvil Press, 2016), and two award-winning poetry chapbooks: *Heirloom Bulldog* (Bright Hill Press, 2015) and *Bonanza* (Slapering Hol Press, 1997). She is widely published, and forthcoming in many journals. (www.lynnmcgee.com)

Rennie McQuilkin served as Connecticut Poet Laureate from 2015-2018. He co-founded the Sunken Garden Poetry Festival, which he directed for nine years. His poetry has appeared in *The Atlantic, Poetry, The American Scholar, The Southern Review, The Yale Review, The Hudson Review*, and other publications. The author of several poetry collections, he has received a number of awards, including fellowships from the NEA and the Connecticut Commission on the Arts, the Connecticut Center for the Book's Lifetime Achievement Award, and its 2010 poetry award. He lives in Bloomfield, Connecticut.

Ilene Millman is a speech/language therapist currently working with preschoolers and volunteering as tutor, tutor trainer, and assessor for her county Literacy Volunteers organization. Her poems have been published in a number of print journals including *The Journal of New Jersey Poets, Nelle, Earth's Daughters, US 1 Worksheets*, and others. She is an associate editor of *The Sow's Ear*. Her first book of poetry, *Adjust Speed to Weather*, was published last year.

Naila Moreira teaches science writing at Smith College and has served as writer in residence at the Shoals Marine Lab in Maine and at the Forbes Library in Northampton, Massachusetts. She is the author of two poetry chapbooks, *Water Street* (Finishing Line Press, 2017), which won the 2018 New England Poetry Society Jean Pedrick Chapbook Prize, and *Gorgeous Infidelities* (Impossible Dream Editions, 2014), an art book in collaboration with internationally recognized photographer Paul Ickovic. Her poetry, fiction, creative nonfiction and journalism have appeared widely. The daughter of Brazilian immigrants who moved to the U.S. when she was five, she has also worked as a journalist, environmental consultant, and Seattle Aquarium docent.

Judith Nacca received an MFA from the University of Massachusetts. Her poetry has been published in *The Massachusetts Review, The Cream City Review, LOCUSPOINT, Cutbank* and *Verse*, among other publications. In 2009, she received an artist fellowship from the Connecticut Commission on Culture and Tourism. As a literacy coach, Nacca nurtures young writers in grades K-4. She resides in Wallingford, Connecticut with her husband, Robert, their daughters, Grace and Sylvia, and their dogs, Suki and Emma.

Patricia Horn O'Brien has worked and volunteered as a social worker throughout her adult life. She's a member of the *Guilford Poets Guild* and co-founded *CT River Poets*. She's helped in the establishment of Prison Hospice in three Connecticut prisons and facilitated poetry workshops at York Correctional Institute. She initiated the ongoing program, *Paintings and Poetry*, at Florence Griswold Museum. O'Brien been published in many periodicals. Her first collection of poetry, *When Less Than Perfect is Enough*, published by Antrim Books, is now in its 2nd printing. Her memoir, written with her son, Richard, was recently published: *The Laughing Rabbit: A Mother, A Son, and the Ties that Bind*. O'Brien is the Poet Laureate of Old Saybrook, Connecticut.

Carla Panciera has published two collections of poetry: *One of the Cimalores* (Cider Press) and *No Day, No Dusk, No Love* (Bordighera). Her collection of short stories, Bewildered, received AWP's 2013 Grace Paley Short Fiction Award. Her work has appeared in several journals including *Poetry, The New England Review, Nimrod*, and others.

Garrett Phelan is the author of the poetry book *Outlaw Odes* (Antrim House 2015) and micro-chapbooks *Unfixed Marks* and *Standing where I am* (Origami Poetry Project 2014 and 2016). His poems have appeared in a variety of publications including *English Potomac Review, Word Riot, Off the Coast, Ekphrasis Review* and *Leaping Clear*. He is a 2017 Pushcart Prize nominee and earned third place in the 2018 Nutmeg Award contest, judged by Ocean Vuong.

Marge Piercy's 19th poetry book is *Made in Detroit*. Her book *The Hunger Moon: New & Selected Poems* was recently published by Knopf. She has written 17 novels; recently *Sex Wars; Dance the Eagle to Sleep, Braide Lives*, and *Vida* were reissued by PM Press, who brought out *The Cost of Lunch, Etc.* (short stories) and *My Life, My Body* (essays, poems, interview). She has appeared in over 500 venues here and abroad, including residences. Her work has been translated into 22 languages. Every June, Piercy runs a juried intensive poetry workshop in Wellfleet, Massachusetts.

Kenneth Pobo has a new book out called *The Antlantis Hit Parade*. His work has appeared in *Mudfish, The Queer South Anthology, Amsterdam Review, Nimrod, Hawaii Review*, and elsewhere.

Bruce Pratt is an award-winning short story writer, poet, and playwright. He is the author of the novel *The Serpents of Blissfull* from Mountain State Press, the poetry collection *Boreal* from Antrim House Books, *The Trash Detail: Stories* from New Rivers Press, and the poetry chapbook *Forms and Shades* from Clare Songbirds Publishing. His fiction, poetry, drama, and essays have appeared in more than forty magazines, reviews, and journals across the United States, and in Canada, Ireland, and Wales. He is the editor of *American Fiction*.

Geri Radacsi is the author of four collections of poetry. Her prize-winning chapbook, *Ancient Music*, was published in 2000 by Pecan Grove Press; her full-length poetry collection, *Trapped in Amber*, appeared in 2005 from Connecticut River Press; *Tightrope Walker* in 2007 by Antrim House, and *Soul and All that Jazz* in 2015 by Finishing Line Press. Radacsi has been a journalist, English teacher, communication/media specialist, and freelance writer. Currently, she is Associate Director of University Relations, Emerita, at Central Connecticut State University in New Britain, Connecticut. She has taught memoir-poetry workshops in Central Connecticut Her poems, choreographed for dance and cello interpretation, have been featured in live performances at CCSU and at the New Britain Museum of American Art.

Charles Rafferty's most recent collections of poems are *The Smoke of Horses* (BOA Editions, 2017) and *Something an Atheist Might Bring Up at a Cocktail Party* (Mayapple Press, 2018). His poems have appeared in *The New Yorker, O, Oprah Magazine, Prairie Schooner,* and *Ploughshares*. His stories have appeared in *The Southern Review* and *New World Writing,* and his story collection is *Saturday Night at Magellan's* (Fomite Press, 2013). He has won grants from the National Endowment for the Arts and the Connecticut Commission on Culture and Tourism, as well as the 2016 NANO Fiction Prize. Currently, he directs the MFA program at Albertus Magnus College and teaches at the Westport Writers' Workshop.

Bruce Robinson's recent work appears in *Mobius, Fourth River/ Tributaries, Pangyrus, Blueline, The Menteur,* and *Spectrum*. He completed his undergraduate studies at Kenyon College and his graduate studies at Johns Hopkins and Toledo.

Amy Schmitz's first poetry collection, *Border Crossing*, was published by the National Federation of State Poetry Societies in 2018. Her work has appeared in many literary journals. Schmitz has won awards from Poetry International, the Women's National Book Association and the CNY chapter of the National League of American Pen Women. She earned an MFA from George Mason University.

Penelope Scambly Schott is a past recipient of the Oregon Book Award for Poetry. Her most recent book is *November Quilt*. "Bless the Old Wheat Farmers" is from a manuscript in progress about a small wheat-growing town in central Oregon.

Natalie Schriefer is currently working towards an MFA in fiction at Southern Connecticut State University, writing a novel that deals with the destructive effects of gender stereotypes. (www.natalieschriefer.com)

Peter Shaver graduated from the University of Scranton in 2018. His poems have been selected for publication in *Esprit, Catfish Creek, the Bridge, Dime Store Review*, and an Arachne Press anthology. He has been awarded the University of Scranton's Berrier Poetry Award and a SCCC Creative Writing Award. He resides in Shavertown, Pennsylvania and works in forestry.

Pegi Deitz Shea is a two-time winner of the Connecticut Book Award for Children's Literature, and author of more than 450 published articles, essays, and poems for adult readers. Her award-winning works for young readers (poetry, articles, fiction and nonfiction picture books, as well as novels) frequently focus on human rights issues. Shea's poetry for adults has appeared in *The Christian Science Monitor, Ireland of the Welcomes Magazine*, and in many other journals and anthologies. Also a photographer, she has had solo exhibits combining poems and pictures. Shea is the founder and director of *Poetry Rocks!*, a quarterly poetry series at Arts Center East in Vernon, Connecticut. She teaches in the Creative Writing Program of the University of Connecticut.

Caroline N. Simpson's chapbook, *Choose Your Own Adventures and Other Poems*, was published by Finishing Line Press in 2018. She has been twice nominated for a Pushcart Prize, both in poetry and nonfiction, and in 2013, a collection of her poetry won Honorable Mention in Hot Street's Emerging Writers Contest. She teaches high school English at the Tatnall School in Wilmington, Delaware, and has taught English literature at international high schools in Turkey and Spain. She loves outdoor adventure, traveling, and learning about other cultures. (www.carolinensimpson.com)

John L. Stanizzi is author of the collections *Ecstasy Among Ghosts, Sleepwalking, Dance Against the Wall, After the Bell, Hallelujah Time!, High Tide – Ebb Tide, Four Bits – Fifty 50-Word Pieces,* and *Chants.* His newest collection, *Sundowning,* will be available soon. His work has been translated into Italian and appeared in *El Ghibli,* in the *Journal of Italian Translations Bonafinni,* and *Poetarium Silva.* For many years, Stanizzi coordinated the *Fresh Voices Poetry Competition* for Young Poets at Hill-Stead Museum in Farmington, Connecticut. He is also a teaching artist for the national recitation contest, *Poetry Out Loud.* A former New England Poet of the Year, John teaches literature at Manchester Community College in Manchester, Connecticut and he lives with his wife, Carol, in Coventry, Connecticut.

Susan Finch Stevens' poems have appeared in various anthologies and journals. Her chapbook *Lettered Bones* was selected by Kwame Dawes as a winner in the South Carolina Poetry Initiative Chapbook Competition. She has served on the board of the Poetry Society of South Carolina for over ten years, including this past year as president. Her handmade artist's books featuring her poetry have been included in both juried and invitational book arts exhibitions. She lives with her husband David and two rambunctious Weimaraners on the Isle of Palms in South Carolina.

Steve Straight's books include *The Almanac* (Curbstone/ Northwestern University Press, 2012) and *The Water Carrier* (Curbstone, 2002). He is professor of English and director of the poetry program at Manchester Community College, in Connecticut.

Tim Suermondt is the author of five full-length poetry collections, including the recent books *The World Doesn't Know You* and *Josephine Baker Swimming Pool.* He has published in *Poetry, Ploughshares, The Georgia Review, Prairie Schooner, Able Muse,* and *Plume,* among many others. He lives in Cambridge with his wife, the poet Pui Ying Wong.

Nancy Swanson is a retired educator living in western North Carolina. She and her husband share four children, a grandchild, and a love of mountain trails. Her poetry has been published in *Broad River Review, Comstock Review, Chattahoochee Review, English Journal,* and *South Carolina Review,* among others. She was the 2018 winner of the Sidney Lanier Poetry Prize.

Aidan VanSuetendael is a recent graduate of Denison University in Granville, Ohio, where she studied poetry and music, graduating with a degree in Creative Writing and a minor in Bluegrass Music. She has written poetry since childhood. In addition to poetry, she also writes music, sings, and plays the banjo in Nashville, Tennessee.

Lee Varon's poetry has been published in various journals and anthologies and nominated for a Pushcart Prize. In 2018, she won the Sunshot Press Poetry Prize for *Shot in the Head.* She is the co-editor of *Spare Change News Poems: An Anthology by Homeless People and Those Touched by Homelessness.* She is a social worker in the Boston area.

Andrew Vogel's poems have appeared in issues of *The Blue Collar Review, The Heartland Review, Spring Street, Off the Coast, The Lehigh Valley Review, Clark Street Review, Slant Poetry Journal, The Evergreen Review, The Green Hills Literary Lantern, The Listening Eye, Plainsongs,* an anthology by Foothills press, and a forthcoming issue of *Parhelion.*

R. Bratten Weiss is an editor, freelance academic, and organic grower residing in rural Ohio. Her creative work has appeared in many literary journals. Her poem "Moonskins," in *Connecticut River Review* 2018, was nominated for a Pushcart. She has a collaborative chapbook, *Mud Woman,* with Joanna Penn Cooper, from Dancing Girl Press (2018). She is completing work on *The Peacemakers,* a literary speculative novel about sex robots, and is seeking publication for *The Dirt,* an eco-gothic novel involving fracking.

Will Wells' most recent poetry collection, *Odd Lots, Scraps & Second-hand, Like New,* won the 2016 Grayson Books Poetry Prize. His previous poetry collection, *Unsettled Accounts,* winner of the Hollis Summers Poetry Prize, was published by Ohio Univ/Swallow Press. An earlier volume of poems, *Conversing with the Light,* won the Anhinga Prize for Poetry.

John Sibley Williams is the author of *As One Fire Consumes Another* (Orison Poetry Prize, 2019), *Skin Memory* (Backwaters Prize, University of Nebraska Press, 2019), *Disinheritance*, and *Controlled Hallucinations*. A nineteen-time Pushcart nominee, Williams is the winner of numerous awards, including the Wabash Prize for Poetry, Philip Booth Award, American Literary Review Poetry Contest, Phyllis Smart-Young Prize, Nancy D. Hargrove Editors' Prize, Confrontation Poetry Prize, and Laux/Millar Prize. He serves as editor of *The Inflectionist Review* and works as a literary agent. He lives in Portland, Oregon.

Martin Willitts Jr. is the author of 24 chapbooks, including the winner of the Turtle Island Quarterly Editor's Choice Award, *The Wire Fence Holding Back the World* (Flowstone Press, 2017), as well as eleven full-length collections including *The Uncertain Lover* (Dos Madres Press, 2018) and *Home Coming Celebration* (FutureCycle Press, 2019).

Connecticut Poetry Society

Join the Connecticut Poetry Society, a state-wide community of poets dedicated to the promotion and enjoyment of poetry. CPS has a long tradition of excellence in publishing work of national and international, as well as Connecticut poets. Our mission is to encourage a community devoted to poetry through chapter meetings, education, and events. You do not need to be a resident of Connecticut to join.

Reap the benefits of CPS membership!

*Free copy of *Connecticut River Review,* a celebrated national poetry journal
*Quarterly CPS Newsletter of current poetry news and events
*Local Chapters for workshop and critique
*Annual Poetry Blast and open mic
*Annual Summer Picnic and open mic
*Annual contests
*Publicity for publications, readings, workshops
*Opportunity to publish poems on CPS website

Visit our website at ctpoetry.net
or email us at connpoetry@comcast.net

Join electronically via our website, or send your name, address, email address, phone, and check for dues ($30 individual, $15 student) made out to CPS to:

CPS Membership
311 Shingle Hill Road
West Haven, CT 06516.

Your membership is renewable in April – National Poetry Month!

Connecticut Poetry Society is a 501c3 organization. Member of The National Federation of State Poetry Societies (NFSPS)

Submission Guidelines for *Connecticut River Review*

Connecticut River Review, a national poetry journal, accepts submissions from February 1 to April 15.

Electronic submissions only: https://connecticutriverreview. submittable.com/

Send up to five pages of poetry on a single document, no more than one poem per page. Include your name on the submission as well as on the submission form. Your cover letter and a brief bio should go on the submission form. Simultaneous submissions are acceptable if we are notified immediately on acceptance elsewhere.

See our website for complete guidelines for the journal and for our annual contests: www.ctpoetry.net.

Ordering *Connecticut River Review*
Connecticut River Review is priced at $15. Shipping and handling is $3. You can get more copies by mail by sending a check made out to CPS or Connecticut Poetry Society to:

CRR
9 Edmund Place
West Hartford, CT 06119

Be sure to clearly state where your order should be sent.

Libraries and other institutions should be able to order *CRR* through Ingram.

CPSIA information can be obtained
at www.ICGtesting.com
Printed in the USA
FSHW021946181119
64265FS